A HEART ON FIRE

A HEART ON FIRE

100 MEDITATIONS ON LOVING YOUR NEIGHBORS WELL

DANIELLE COKE BALFOUR

Andrews McMeel
PUBLISHING®

To my family, whose love keeps my heart open,
and to my husband, Cody, whose love
fans my heart's flames.

DON'T LET YOUR HEART GROW COLD.
THE WORLD NEEDS ITS WARMTH.
WITH EVERY BEAT, LIFE FLOWS OUT—
ALL THAT YOU DO WILL ERUPT FROM
THAT DEEP WELL. WHEN THE
TRAGEDIES OF THIS LIFE PIERCE
YOUR HEART LIKE ICE, LET
THEM BE MET BY THE WARMTH OF
COMPASSION, THE HEAT OF LOVE
IN MOTION. MAY YOUR HEART
SWELL WITH A DESIRE TO REMEMBER
ALL THAT IS TRUE, AND RIGHT, AND
LOVELY, AND JUST. LET YOUR DAYS BE
THE EVIDENCE OF A HEART ON FIRE.
-DANIELLE COKE BALFOUR

TEN PILLARS OF A

LOVE

CREATIVITY

JUSTICE

HOPE

AWARENESS

LIFE OF GOOD WORK

COMMUNITY

CONSISTENCY

EMPATHY

HONESTY

REDEMPTION

A life well-lived requires a firm foundation.

The sturdiest and most long-lasting buildings were not created by accident. They are often the result of months and years of meticulous planning, preparation, and construction. When considering how a building will stand the test of time, we look to its base. What keeps it standing tall? How is it fortified?

The journey of good work is undertaken by individuals who know what they stand for. Their values and beliefs are laid brick-by-brick, cemented together by an unwavering dedication to living these values out loud. The Ten Pillars of a Life of Good Work laid before you in this book are merely a snippet of the shared belief systems that collectively prop us up and hold us together. The values of love, creativity, justice, hope, awareness, community, consistency, empathy, honesty, and redemption are a few of the pillars that hold my life up and create a firm foundation for my pursuit of human flourishing.

Solid groundwork helps us weather storms, survive attacks, and stand strong in the face of adversity. As you seek to live with a heart on fire, let the meditations found within these pages help you fortify what you stand for.

TABLE OF

CONTENTS

YOUR HEART IS A WELL OF LIFE

Your Heart, the Well

What do you yearn for? In the stillness, when your heart seems to lunge forward in your chest, what is it moving toward? Your heart is a well. It's deep and wide, filled with goodness and complexity. It's a powerful force that leads your life. What do you enjoy most? Whom do you love? Which convictions guide you? What are your beliefs?

Each one of us has been placed in a unique context. The people we're surrounded by, the places we go, the city we live in, and the things we go through have shaped us in specific ways. It's in this context we can find the mission we've been put on Earth to fulfill.

Let this fill you with excitement for a moment. You—exactly as you are—have been equipped to impact this world in beautiful ways simply because you exist. The experiences you've had and obstacles you've overcome have become tools tucked into your belt, ready to be wielded for the good of another.

Even so, a mission identified will inevitably become a mission interrupted. Feelings of guilt, inadequacy, fear, and countless other intimidating emotions will be no stranger to you. Your guiding light, your reminder that you were made for this, will be your beating heart. It says to you: "You're alive! This matters to you! This is at the core of who you are!" And when life's circumstances seek to suffocate you, may all of the goodness in you erupt and bubble over, scorching every lie with the truth of your power.

Let your mission set you ablaze. Burn so brightly that injustice and oppression cannot slink about in the darkness unscathed. Allow the deep well of your heart to fill to the brim with all of the good you can do and live your life in the overflow.

The Ultimate Good

One of the most beautifully complex feelings that we experience on Earth is the feeling of loving and being loved in return. It's alive, taking on many different forms and functions. It's calling our loved ones to make sure they got home safely, or a home-cooked meal for the family at the end of a long day. It's the flutter in our hearts when we lock eyes with our beloved.

As special as it is to experience, love also asks something of us. It quietly knocks at our heart's door and whispers, "There is more to me than a fluttery feeling." While love leads us to wish for the good of those around us, it also requires actively working for their well-being too.

Love is more than desire; it's also a powerful tool. It's what pushes us to take action on behalf of those who need us most, whether that be through volunteering our time, donating our resources, speaking up for positive change, or encouraging someone in a tough season. Love does not allow others to be consistently marred by the horrors of injustice; it intervenes. Love says, "Yes, this is uncomfortable, but because I love you, I must see this through."

This love is unconditional—whole, full, complete, no strings attached. It's the embodiment of the divine. It pushes and pulls, moving us to live beyond ourselves and reminding us that we belong to one another.

Seeking out the ultimate good for others requires this kind of love—one that propels us into wishing and working for the best outcome in others' lives, as much as we are able. Unconditional love liberates. It is living, breathing, and active, and it's calling to each of us. May our lives be the answer to the knock at our heart's door.

Love of Neighbor

What does it mean to love your neighbor? For the unhoused neighbor, love might look like a smile of acknowledgment or a place to shelter for the night. For the neighbor who owns a small business, it can look like a supporting purchase or leaving a positive review after a season of uncertainty. But in the face of the difficulties we're navigating as a global community—hatred, racism, political tension, health crises, and so many others—many of us look to our left and right and ask ourselves, "How am I supposed to love my neighbor now?"

The solution lies not in the "how" but in our definition of neighborly love. Too often, people use the phrase "love your neighbor" as a passive way to avoid tension instead of the transformative force it's meant to be. This lifeless love seeks peace without justice and unity without accountability. It mimics patience and kindness without continuing forward to protect and persevere. Instead of divine love that seeks out and rejoices in truth, this watered-down love coddles injustice and avoids tension.

The love we are called to share with our neighbor is unconditional, and it shines most brightly in the darkness of despair, injustice, and hate. It's the love Dr. Martin Luther King Jr. spoke of when describing it as the universe's greatest force. This love brings heaven down to Earth.

How do we live out this kind of love? By seeking truth at the expense of our own comfort. We acknowledge the hard things, take sacrificial action, and hold space for others. It requires a commitment to faithfully pursue all that is good, even when it's uncomfortable.

This love is not tolerance; it's transformation. It looks into the pit of darkness and declares, "I will not rest until the light of truth shines through." This love never fails.

lies get
LOUD,
but love is
LOUDER

When Lies Get Loud

There are moments when life's circumstances convince us that we're invisible. Hardships and difficulties back us into dark corners, smothering us with lies of unworthiness and hiding us from the light of what is true. We look around and tell ourselves that we are not seen, that our struggles are mere annoyances to others, and that we are no worse off than the next person.

Even when you do not see it, you must know that someone is wishing and working for your good. You are a treasure, a vital piece of life's puzzle. You are worth loving because you are here. When the lies get loud, drown them out with the truth.

You are not invisible. While your circumstances may create feelings of isolation and loneliness, remember that you are not alone. Recall moments of joy, connection, and belonging. Lean into those relationships and experiences that make you feel alive. See yourself for who you are: treasured and worthy.

You are not a nuisance. You don't have to belittle your own experiences or make yourself small so as to not take up much space. What happened to you matters. You deserve connections that make space for you to exist fully and honestly. Keep searching for safe spaces until you find them, and allow healing to flow through you until you begin to feel whole again.

You do not need to compare your experiences to the next person. Your life is not a competition. Regardless of what someone else is going through, the hardships you face in your life are valid and real. Each of us lives in our own contexts, measured by our own scales; to compare our struggles to that of another would be impossible. Draw strength and connection from those who've tread similar paths, but know that your path is your own.

You are seen, known, and loved. Lies get loud, but love is louder.

TRUE ACTS OF LOVE

SOLIDARITY IN
THE PURSUIT OF
DISMANTLING
UNJUST SYSTEMS

EMPATHY AND
CONNECTION WHEN
WALKING THROUGH
ROUGH SEASONS

THE GIFT OF
INTENTIONAL TIME
SPENT TOGETHER

WORDS THAT SPEAK
TRUTH AND CALL OUT
HARMFUL RHETORIC

ENCOURAGEMENT TO
KEEP GOING WHEN
TIMES ARE DIFFICULT

AWARENESS OF
THREATS TO
FLOURISHING AND
QUALITY OF LIFE

Public Displays of Affection

Could it be that your public works show off whom you call "beloved"?

I fell in love for the first time in 2021. My now husband, Cody, swept me off my feet almost immediately and showed me what it felt like to be truly treasured, thought about, and listened to. I wasn't used to being showered with affection in public by someone I was dating, and it felt foreign to me for a while. It even surprised me to see how eager he was to tell his loved ones about me. In time, I grew to understand these actions as his way of reminding me of his love toward me.

Whether it thrills you or leaves you with secondhand embarrassment, public displays of affection often communicate desire and pride. These actions identify one's beloved and demonstrate a boldness to show them off. Similarly, the work we do for justice functions as a show of who we love and what we value.

Most of us do not seek to do justice simply because it's the right thing to do. Working for justice is a desire born out of love for our fellow humans. This love is on display whenever we take steps to act on behalf of others. A love that takes place behind closed doors has the appearance of intimacy, but if it's never able to be publicly acknowledged or shared with others, the intimacy can quickly morph into secrecy and become clouded with shame. We'd ask, "Do you not love me enough to tell others about me?"

Justice shouts love from the rooftops. It's a declaration of our affections—proof of whom we love and how much we love them. If we're never moved to demonstrate that love with public works, it begs the question: am I truly loving others?

TOOLS THAT LOVE EQUIPS US WITH

VULNERABILITY

COMPASSION

DEDICATION

POWER

FREEDOM

PURPOSE

GROWTH

ENERGY

COURAGE

Strength in Weakness

It's been said that love is weakness. We see this sentiment echoed in fairy tales and stories of superheroes: the courageous main character comes face-to-face with their "damsel in distress" or loved one in peril and engages in some kind of self-sacrificial act to rescue and protect them. The loved one exposes the protagonist's soft spot or point of weakness the "bad guy" can take advantage of.

The sentiment of love as weakness can show up in our changemaking efforts in different ways. Bringing up love as a concept in conversations for progress can be seen as too soft or idealistic. Some say, "It's not love we want; it's change! We want to dismantle structures, not hold hands and sing." Love can sound weak in comparison to cries for justice. And, in a society with a history of destroying and excluding certain people groups, having any kind of "soft spot" can feel risky.

As those beloved fairy tales reach their conclusions, we see that the hero rises up to defeat the evildoer and that love conquers all. In the face of adversity, love musters up some kind of internal strength that bursts out and eliminates the foe. For those of us who desire to defeat the enemies of injustice and hate, we, too, can be energized from the power of our love for each other. When we see people wrongfully imprisoned, suffering under poverty, or being discriminated against, our love for them is the match that ignites the fire of action within us, pushing us to fight for justice.

Love can make us vulnerable. It exists like targets on our backs, pointing out to oppressors exactly where to strike. Yet there's a beauty that unleashes when we draw from that same love as a source of power. Love keeps our eyes fixed on what we're fighting for. And, when it's time for battle, love becomes our greatest weapon.

A POSTURE OF INTENTIONALITY
BRINGING LOVE TO OTHERS

alleviate
STRESS

respect
SPACE

honor
CAPACITY

Bringing Love to Others

One day, a lovely human sent me a message on Instagram describing how her friends intentionally brought love into her space during a difficult time. It was her birthday, and she was being cautious because of the pandemic, so she didn't make any plans to gather. To her surprise, her friends showed up in her driveway and left gifts for her.

How encouraging and practical. A global pandemic can certainly dampen any birthday celebration, but these friends took a moment to make her day special while honoring her desire to keep safe and distant.

When aiming to bring love to someone else, maintaining a mindset of intentionality is both honoring and respectful. It involves taking another person's wants and needs into consideration, not just doing what we think is best for them. An intentional person thinks, "I could send them groceries or find out if it's best to send some prepared meals instead." Both are kind, thoughtful gestures, but a posture of intentionality asks us to seek out acts of love that best fit another's situation.

Intentionality also matters when bringing love to strangers. What good is a donation of dirty, ripped clothing to a community drive? Is it honoring to give of scraps and waste? Intentionality involves giving with respect to the needs of others, not just making ourselves feel good by offloading our leftovers.

When we practice intentionality and dignity, we preserve the autonomy of others while still working for their good.

I'M SPENDING LESS TIME PULLING THEIR WEEDS

AND MORE TIME TENDING TO MY FLOWERS

Let Your Days Be the Evidence

Our love for others often revs up the desire to recruit them to the "good side." When our heart swells with the realization of all that is true, right, and just, we want the overflow to spill out onto everyone around us, hoping to set their hearts ablaze too. Yet we often find that this is an uphill battle. We discover that behind staunch opinions are a collection of closely held beliefs propping them up—and the work it takes to dismantle these beliefs in others is ultimately not ours to do.

The truth is, it is not your responsibility to convince anyone of anything, nor are you tasked with changing someone else's mind. The thoughts and actions of others are ultimately outside of your control. Does this mean that you don't try to help others see something from your perspective? Not at all. Conversations are critical, yet at the same time, there is only so much you can do.

What's next? We don't want to give up on our loved ones, marking them as lost causes who will never see things the way we do, yet we don't want to consistently launch ourselves headfirst into a wall that won't budge. Instead, consider taking that energy and redirecting it inward. Focus on cultivating and nurturing your own belief system and the consistent dedication to living out your own beliefs.

Instead of exerting all of your energy trying to convince someone of a truth you hold dear, spend more time living a life that exemplifies your values in a way that makes it difficult to refute the power of your perspective.

If, at the end of your life, you look back and realize that you were never successful in changing the minds of your friends, I hope the evidence of a life well-lived speaks loudly on your behalf, and that your legacy shows just how much you loved your neighbors.

LITTLE WAYS TO LOVE

30 DAYS OF LIVING OUT LOVE IN SMALL, MEANINGFUL WAYS

GIVE A COMPLIMENT THAT GOES BEYOND THE SURFACE	CONGRATULATE SOMEONE ON A MEANINGFUL ACCOMPLISHMENT	CALL SOMEONE WHO'S NOT EXPECTING TO HEAR FROM YOU TODAY
SEND SOMEONE A FEW DOLLARS FOR A CUP OF COFFEE	FIND A NEW ORGANIZATION TO SUPPORT	WRITE A LETTER AND SEND IT TO A LOVED ONE
HOLD THE DOOR OPEN FOR A FEW MORE PEOPLE THAN YOU NORMALLY WOULD	LEARN TWO WORDS IN SIGN LANGUAGE	ADD A FEW PEOPLE'S BIRTHDAYS TO YOUR CALENDAR
REMIND SOMEONE OF HOW MUCH THEY MEAN TO YOU	SEND A FUNNY MEME OR VIDEO TO A FRIEND	LEAVE A POSITIVE REVIEW ONLINE FOR ONE OF YOUR FAVORITE RESTAURANTS
START A LIST OF YOUR FRIENDS' FAVORITE THINGS	INTRODUCE YOURSELF TO SOMEONE YOU'VE BEEN WANTING TO CONNECT WITH	FIND AN ETHICAL WAY TO DONATE YOUR LIGHTLY USED CLOTHING

EACH DAY PRESENTS YOU WITH UNIQUE OPPORTUNITIES TO SHOW LOVE THROUGH SHOWING UP FOR OTHERS. HERE ARE A FEW WAYS TO INTENTIONALLY PRACTICE A LIFE OF PRESENCE AND CARE.

SEND A FRIEND A QUOTE THAT REMINDS YOU OF THEM	TAKE A TASK OFF OF A LOVED ONE'S PLATE WHO NEEDS MARGIN	GIVE A HUG THAT LASTS A LITTLE LONGER THAN USUAL
LEAVE A STICKY NOTE WITH A FEW NICE WORDS FOR ANOTHER PERSON TO FIND	WRITE A KIND COMMENT ON A SMALL BUSINESS OWNER'S SOCIAL MEDIA POST	SEND SOMEONE A SONG THAT REMINDS YOU OF THEM
CHECK UP ON A FRIEND WHO'S BEEN GOING THROUGH A HARD TIME	SMILE AT THE NEXT PERSON YOU SEE	WRITE DOWN FIVE THINGS YOU'RE GRATEFUL FOR
GRAB TWO EXTRA ITEMS TO DONATE NEXT TIME YOU GO TO THE STORE	TOSS LITTER INTO THE NEAREST GARBAGE BIN	FIND A PETITION ONLINE FOR AN IMPORTANT CAUSE AND SIGN IT
TRY NOT TO PICK UP YOUR PHONE DURING YOUR NEXT FACE-TO-FACE CONVERSATION	LEARN A NEW FACT ABOUT A CAUSE THAT MATTERS TO YOU	LET SOMEONE GO IN FRONT OF YOU IN LINE

Dear you,

Do you believe that you're worthy of the love you give?

I see the way you pour out for those around you and I've witnessed the lengths you go to make others feel like they belong. You help others shoulder the weight of their hardships, you give of your time and resources, and you often put others before yourself.

Did you know that it's okay to choose yourself too?

We live in a world where self-love is either demonized completely or the sum of one's full focus. For the absolute giver, love of self is merely a distraction—seen as an idolatrous focus on one's own life and gain. For the absolute taker, love of self is the only necessity—the sole priority at all times and seen as a form of protection and insulation from the world's hardships and attacks.

To experience love fully, you'll need to find the balance between healthy self-regard and consideration for others. Give of yourself while also taking note of when your cup is running low. Care for yourself while also setting aside time and effort to show up for others. The two areas do not compete—they complement and fuel each other, creating a necessary balance for a life of love and impact.

You are worthy of the love you give. In your choosing of others, it's okay to choose yourself. You only get one life with your steady, beating heart. Lean into it for compassion and kindness, but protect it from callousness and selfishness.

As you spend your days giving me away, don't forget to come home to me too.

With love,
Your heart ♡

CREAT

Made to Be a Maker

When the word "creativity" comes to mind for most people, they instantly envision paintbrushes, colored pencils, and Picasso. The concept of creativity is often reserved for the artists, poets, and musicians among us, and it's rare for the everyday person to see themselves in this light. Many never realize that there are, in the twists and turns of our own journeys, countless opportunities to discover how to uniquely live out a meaningful, creative life.

Let's settle this once and for all: you are a maker. You are creative by nature. When you get up in the morning, you *make* your bed. No, you probably didn't build it, but you arrange it—you put it together and prepare it. You also make your schedule, your coffee, and your morning routine. Each day is brought to life by a collection of choices that you *make*.

I define creativity as taking something and *making* it into something else. Yes, this is demonstrated by artists, engineers, and chefs, but it's also done by problem-solvers, thinkers, listeners, and helpers. The world needs people who will use what they have to build something better. This kind of making requires no specific skill or talent, just a willing heart and ready hands. You can start today by identifying how you already spend your days and finding ways to inject moments of magic into them—for you and for the world around you. Create a life that consistently churns out beauty.

Make gift baskets filled with baby items for new mothers in need. Make decisions on which policies you'll support in local elections. Make time to sit with someone and offer a shoulder to lean on in times of need. Make moments of learning and nurturing for the little ones in your life.

Make do with what you have—more often than not, that's more than enough.

WHAT I'M GOOD AT

SKILLS ST

THINGS THAT COME
MOST NATURALLY TO ME

AREAS I'M
PROFICIENT IN

CAUSES CT

THINGS THAT
OTHERS SAY
I DO WELL

ISSUES THAT
MAKE ME COME
ALIVE

PRESENT
PURPOSE

INJUSTICES THAT
I'M PERSONALLY
AFFECTED BY OR
CONNECTED TO

AREAS OF INTEREST

PASSIONS PL

TOPICS I'M
KNOWLEDGEABLE
ON

THINGS I DEEPLY
CARE ABOUT

DREAMS THAT
KEEP ME UP
AT NIGHT

Discovering Present Purpose

Has the idea of purpose ever intimidated you? Sometimes the pressure to discover the "one thing" you're meant to do with your *entire* life can be overwhelming. A simpler way to lean into the concept is to discover your *present* purpose: what you're meant to do right now. When you grant yourself the grace to stumble down the paths of exploring your passions, honing your skills, and identifying your causes, you're able to piece together what purpose can look like in any season, step by step.

Passion can be found in the things that make our hearts come alive, the topics that we know inside out, and the dreams that keep us up at night. Passions stir deeply within us. They swell up inside our hearts until we feel like we'll burst and compel us to act in one way or another. Down this path, we find what we love most.

Our skills are the abilities we possess that cause us to shine brightly in areas that may be dim for others. Skills don't just help us land day jobs; they reveal opportunities to do the most good in ways that feel most natural. Down this path, we find what we do best.

The list of causes to care about runs long in a world overrun with injustice. While your passions or life experiences may bring you face-to-face with society's greatest needs, it's your resolve to do something about those needs that leads you to adopt a cause and own it. Down this path, we find ways to right wrongs.

At the intersection of these three paths lies the opportunity to shape a life of purpose. By creatively combining these facets of our personal journeys, we can use what we're made of to discover what we're made for.

Perfectly Imperfect

I often call myself a recovering perfectionist. I'm no stranger to bearing the weight of my mistakes, unfinished to-do lists, and unmet goals. In sharing my art and other creative pursuits, it's tempting to want to highlight the "good" and leave out all of the hardships that often come along with it. I didn't realize that hiding behind the appearance of perfection was doing a disservice to my life experience and the people around me who crave connection and authenticity.

Imperfection is one thing in life we all have in common. The sooner imperfection is accepted and embraced, the more quickly we can share beauty with our one, precious life. When we lay down the pretense of perfection, we free ourselves to truly experience the reality of our humanity and remind others that their imperfections are normal. Our authenticity shows others that they are worthy of pursuing what they love, too, even in the midst of not having all the answers.

Imperfection sheds light on areas that need growth. Paying attention to the ways we fall short opens our eyes to ways we can become more loving, patient, kind, and compassionate. How would we develop if we were set on pretending faults and imperfections did not exist within ourselves?

At the end of the day, imperfection reminds us that in some ways, we won't ever "get it all done." Whether it's an unhealthy habit, an unfinished painting, or hope unfulfilled, we will look back on our lives and see something left incomplete. This is as it should be—not for a lack of trying, but because it's beyond our human nature to do everything perfectly. What we have instead is an opportunity to walk in authenticity, knowing that we can only do so much and that whatever gift we offer the world is a gift worth giving.

CHARACTERISTICS OF CHANGEMAKERS

THE ABILITY TO IDENTIFY BROKEN SYSTEMS

THE COURAGE TO TEAR THEM DOWN

THE IMAGINATION TO DREAM OF A NEW WAY FORWARD

THE STRENGTH TO TRY TO BUILD A BETTER FUTURE

Characteristics of Changemakers

One of the most overlooked attributes of a true changemaker is the gift of reimagination: the ability to take what you have, reflect on what's been done before, and conjure up a new, refreshing conception of what life could look like. This skill is an art form requiring honesty, hope, and courage, yet the road to reimagination is paved with many other necessary steps.

First, a changemaker must possess the ability to identify broken systems. It's one thing to be able to point out all that's wrong with the world, but another thing entirely to look past any "fruit" and identify rotten roots. It takes an investigative listener—one who hears feedback and peels back layers—to discover what's underneath. This process is how we decide where change should take place.

Second, a changemaker must have the courage to tear down broken systems. This means cutting, pruning, and uprooting. It takes a brave person to willingly destroy entire structures with the intention of establishing something new in their place.

Along these lines, a changemaker has the ability to dream and envision a new way forward. This is the recreation and reimagining process filled with trial and error, but also with hope and calculated efforts. They learn from the mistakes of the past and apply the wisdom gained from those who came before them, allowing prior discoveries to inform the current work.

These are no easy tasks. Changemakers require strength to try to build a better future. Their work involves testing new systems, analyzing what does and doesn't work, and going back to the drawing board for the good of the communities they serve.

Demolition is a spectacle. Many show up for the tearing down of what's wrong, but few hang around for the building up of what's right. Changemakers see things through 'til the end—reimagining a future full of collective thriving and working to make it come to pass.

I AM MORE THAN WHAT I MAKE

I AM FREE TO CREATE AND RELEASE

You Are Not What You Do

For those of us who seek to live a meaningful life, it's easy to fall into the trap of defining ourselves by the works of our hands. Crafting a life of purpose and intention often blurs the distinction between who we are and what we do. If we're not careful, the gray area can lead to an internalization of failure, a lack of rest, and a deep-seated feeling of never doing—or being—enough.

The maker must develop a healthy sense of detachment from what is made—not in a way that leads you to churn out works devoid of life and meaning, but in a way that prevents you from tying up your identity with those works. An article not getting many views online does not make the author unworthy or unseen. A missed note in a musical performance does not make the musician incapable.

When your identity is tied up in what you produce, criticism can feel like a blow to the chest. Every failure felt to the core; every mistake a mark on your character. Rest evades you, even when you're on the brink of burnout, because a pause in production feels like a pause in life's meaning. You're unable to see your worth separate from your work.

Maintain a healthy space between your creations and your core, but let your core continue to inform your creations. You can hold them close without keeping them tethered to your identity. In this new relationship, you won't be swept away with praise or smothered by critique, feeling the weight of both but being defined by neither. You are free to create for the sake of expressing yourself—no strings attached.

BRING ALL OF YOU TO ALL YOU DO!

THE INGREDIENTS OF YOUR UNIQUE CONTRIBUTION

SPHERE AND COMMUNITY

CULTURE

KNOWLEDGE

HOBBIES

STORY

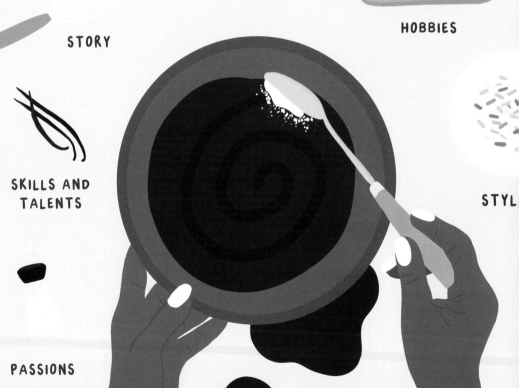

SKILLS AND TALENTS

STYL

PASSIONS

Your Unique Contribution

Believe it or not, even if there are a million people already doing what you want to do, what you bring to the world is completely unique. There may be plenty of activists, artists, teachers, doctors, librarians, counselors, and entrepreneurs, but the world only has one of you. Here are three reasons why you can do what someone else is already doing and still offer a completely unique contribution to the world:

Your original ideas, artistic flair, internal rhythms, sources of inspiration—all of these are uniquely yours. It's the upward stroke you use with your pen or the way the wheels turn in your mind as you brainstorm. The more you trust yourself and hone your skills, the more you will step into your own and cultivate your personal style.

The hardships you've overcome, mountains you've climbed, experiences you've been shaped by—all of these are uniquely yours. Maybe a loss in your childhood has led you to dedicate your life to mental health awareness, or a chronically ill family member has stoked your desire to fight for the cure of a disease. The causes you're passionate about are inextricably linked to the life you've lived, and both profoundly influence the work you do.

The cultures that influence you, the places you spend the most time, the people you call home—all of these are uniquely yours. Consider where you spend your time on a daily, weekly, or even monthly basis. You have an immense amount of influence in these places, even when it doesn't feel that way. Your coworkers, your family, and your community are the mission you're called to, and no two missions are the same.

The next time you're tempted to shrink because you see others doing similar work, remember that nobody else can do what you're called to do in the ways that you've been called to do it. Your contribution is uniquely yours—and the world waits to see what you do next.

CREATIVE OPPORTUNITIES
FOUND IN CHAOS

A REMINDER OF WHAT GUIDES US AND MATTERS MOST IN THIS LIFE

THE ABILITY TO IDENTIFY AREAS THAT NEED REPAIR AND IMPROVEMENT

A CHANCE TO USE OUR GIFTS FOR HOPE AND HEALING

COLLECTIVE INSPIRATION THAT COMES FROM A SHARED STRUGGLE WITH OTHERS

A SHARPENED FOCUS AS A RESULT OF CONSTRAINTS

Creating in Chaos

For many of us, the last few years of pandemics, racial reckonings, and political unrest have left us standing in what feels like the aftermath of a powerful storm. With rubble and debris everywhere, we scratch our heads, wondering how in the world we're going to rebuild. Where do we go from here?

It's been said that creativity thrives in constraint. When we're short on time, low on context, or limited with our supplies, we can find ourselves suddenly motivated to churn out our best work. Yet what happens when the limits imposed on us go beyond our work and extend to our whole lives? How can we create when the troubles of life have rocked us to the core?

Writers like Toni Morrison and James Baldwin remind us that times of trouble are when the world needs our creativity most of all. Yes, our artwork and writings can breathe new life and hope into the hearts and minds of those who engage with it, but beyond that, our creativity sparks problem-solving strategies that can help us repair and improve society.

We must rise to the challenge of resisting hopelessness, and instead, be inspired to dream up creative solutions for human flourishing, both during and after the chaos. Continuing in the face of turmoil requires us to channel our faith and hope into our good work, not for the sake of productivity, but to flood the world with enough beauty and truth to trigger collective healing.

To create in the aftermath or the middle of hardship requires incredible tenacity and strength. When we persevere and use our gifts to meet the moment, we create landmarks that we can point back to and guideposts to light the way for those who will follow in our footsteps.

SMALL THINGS THAT
ACTUALLY MATTER A LOT

**A PIECE THAT
COMPLETES A PUZZLE**

**A BRIGHT IDEA
THAT BRINGS CHANGE**

**A SNOWFLAKE THAT
SETS OFF AN AVALANCE**

**THE STRIKE OF A MATCH
THAT STARTS A FIRE**

**A STAR THAT'S PART
OF A CONSTELLATION**

**A DOMINO THAT TRIGGERS
A CHAIN REACTION**

Chain Reaction

Your "little" means a lot.

It's easy to look at your own talents, ideas, or contributions and question how much they really matter. In the grand scheme of things, is there much value in the good that you bring?

The volume of contributions happening around the world should not cause you to look at your own offering with disappointment. Rather, hold up your offering in the light and see that, just like the rest of us, you have a place.

A puzzle piece is not insignificant on its own, no matter how small. It was created to be viewed in combination with all the rest. That does not eliminate its value, but magnifies it, for its beauty shines brighter when it is present and serves its purpose.

It only takes one domino to knock down all the others in a beautiful chain reaction. Yet the domino on its own has value and its absence would be noticed. The flames of our fireplace warm the whole home, yet the match is more than enough to light a sweet-smelling candle's wick.

Sharing your gifts with the world creates a joy that's twofold. Like a star in the night sky, we get to experience your brilliance as you choose to shine, and we also get to behold the magnificence of you joining in with other stars around you as you form glorious constellations.

In times of hurt and pain, we need goodness wherever it can be found. When you shine your light in one dark corner, you join with others who do the same and eventually light up the world around you. This is the work that matters. Your "little" is more than enough.

THIS IS GROWTH

THIS IS GROWTH

My story...

THIS IS PROGRESS

MY STORY

THIS IS PROGRESS

THIS IS ART

THIS IS ART

The Art of the In-Between

It's not unusual for a creator to be solely concerned with the completed work. The goal of many creative sessions is to work toward an end: like a finished poem, stunning portrait, or delicious dessert. We'd like our work to be seen in the best possible light—completed, polished, and ready for consumption. Because of this desire, we often miss out on the beauty of the in-between.

This can also be true in our daily endeavors. We are constantly in the middle of life's many processes: self-improvement, parenting, advocacy, spirituality, relationships, and more. We consistently work on ourselves, viewing success only as crossing the finish line of our goals. Yet it's the journey along the way—the challenges we overcome, little lessons we learn, and ways we grow—that's worth celebrating too.

The in-between is where we most often exist. The larger hopes and benchmarks that we set for ourselves often aren't achievable in a day, a week, or even a month. Books can take years to write, and relationships can take just as long to grow and progress. It's in celebrating the in-between that we breathe life into our day-to-day existence, not viewing ourselves as constant self-improvement projects, but as human beings with worth and value, no matter how many items we check off of life's to-do list.

We live into the beauty of the in-between by acknowledging our daily progress. If the masterpiece you're working on has one more painted section than it did yesterday, you've created art. If you had that difficult conversation you've been dreading for weeks, you've beautifully progressed. Each day you've worked toward a goal or dream matters, even with missteps and imperfect moments.

We can't wait 'til the end to enjoy the journey. Fall in love with the in-between. Those messy bits, the spilled paint, and the missed spots. It's not just art when you finish. It was art when you began.

You've always been a masterpiece.

ADVENTURE AWAITS.

Your Blank Page

I welcome a clean slate. Whether it's the turning of a page in a journal, a blank canvas, or a new season, there's something inviting and hopeful about an open space not stained with memory or mistakes.

Your days are filled with chances to welcome the newness of a blank page. The more you recognize this, the more you'll view each moment as a grace-filled opportunity to do a new thing. Blank pages can be a chance for a fresh start, a way to give yourself white space, or a pathway to exploration.

A fresh start is often the imagery that comes to mind when initially thinking about a clean slate. From new year celebrations to the first day at a new school, we welcome change as a chance to start over. The good news is, you don't have to be walking through a major life change to give yourself the opportunity to turn a new page. With every breath, you're consistently being offered a way to begin anew. Start over as often as you need to.

A blank page can also come in the form of white space. In design, we learn that white spaces are those necessary gaps and breaks in words, graphics, or lines that give the design breathing room. White space doesn't always occur naturally; it's tempting to want to fill every inch of the page with something, but that can result in overwhelming the design and making it difficult for the viewer to interact with it. The same can be said about our days. Factoring white space into our lives means giving ourselves margin and room to breathe. It's choosing to not pack every minute with tasks or obligations, but rather inject moments of rest and slowness into our full and chaotic days.

The most curious use of a blank page can be found in exploration. I commonly reach for a fresh sheet of computer paper when I experience lightbulb moments or want to unpack a bright, new idea. Blank pages are opportunities to get messy—to unload our thoughts and experiment without rules or reason.

Whatever a blank page means for you, find moments to explore the opportunities found in those quiet, empty spaces.

TICE

INJUSTICE BLOCKS THE WAY

DOING JUSTICE CLEARS THE PATH

Let Justice Roll Down

At the core of our existence lies the concept of justice. It exists on a continuum, an ever-flowing standard of fairness, correctness, and morality. It rolls down, as the Scriptures say, like waters, and we ourselves are called to be its conduits. Justice uninterrupted creates harmony, equality, and peace.

Driven by a desire for power, humans often take matters into their own hands. We construct dams that deter the flow of justice in our societies, building up reservoirs of harm, greed, and privilege. Injustice obstructs—depriving people and communities of the resources they need to thrive and making them more susceptible to mistreatment and ruin.

To do justice in society is to clear the path so all that's good and right can flow through. Where injustice breaks and impedes, we actively seek repair and restoration. Where access to this flowing river is limited, our good works are like wells, bringing relief to those who need it.

We ourselves are not the originators of justice. It exists outside of us. Yet we have an opportunity—a responsibility—to tap into this great river and funnel it into the places and spaces that have long been dried out.

Our work to do justice should be twofold. Collectively, we must remove all that blocks its path. This takes reforming systems, changing laws, holding people accountable, and revitalizing communities. It's the active destruction of the dams. Although necessary, this process can be long and difficult. This is why the work must also be personal: on the ground and in the weeds. It's community initiatives, restored relationships, and supporting the vulnerable. These are the wells.

Justice will always flow. In those places where it seems scarce, let us be the vessels through which it seeps out.

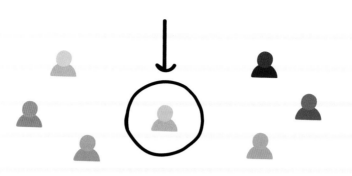

AN UNJUST SOCIETY CENTERS THE PRIVILEGED

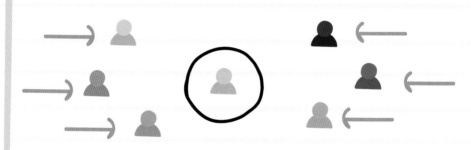

GOOD WORK REACHES FOR THOSE ON THE MARGINS

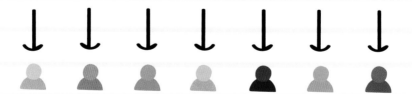

A JUST SOCIETY FAIRLY DISTRIBUTES POWER AND RESOURCES

Meet Me at the Margins

In design, one thing I've learned to focus on is the placement of margins. These lines confine the main content of a design or body of text to the middle of a page, assisting with layout and readability. Another type of margin—bleed—is used to ensure that all important elements of a design are kept within a "safe area," protected from being cut off during the printing process. Everything valuable should be put as close to the center as possible.

Society was structured to prioritize those at the center too. The closer you find yourself to the socially constructed "norms" of white, male, straight, and affluent, the more protected and valued you are. Those who do not fit this template are pushed out further and further to the edges—the margins—where they're susceptible to being cut off from life's necessities and privileges. This illuminates the heart behind the work: the margins are our mission.

The work of the margins is often muffled by the noise of polarization. In an effort to not get caught up in the mess of it all, many of us choose a different kind of "center," one that attempts to keep the peace by not choosing a side. While alluring, this kind of centrism falls short if the needs of those on the outskirts of society aren't considered. Good work doesn't settle for the comfort of the middle ground.

The way forward is toward the margins. It's a way that centers those in need among us, and actually works for their good in all ways—from politics to their front porch and everything in between. While we aim to make the excluded the center of our focus, our top priority is not to bring them to the center of our societal constructs. Instead, we seek to liberate all of us from the structures and systems that have marginalized some of us in the first place—until all are protected and none are cut away.

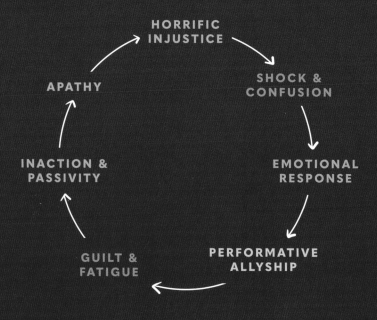

HORRIFIC
INJUSTICE

SHOCK &
CONFUSION

APATHY

EMOTIONAL
RESPONSE

INACTION &
PASSIVITY

GUILT &
FATIGUE

PERFORMATIVE
ALLYSHIP

THE CYCLE OF ~~IN~~ACTION

SO, WHEN
HORRIFIC
INJUSTICE
TAKES PLACE,

WE WON'T BE
OVERTAKEN BY
SHOCK &
CONFUSION
AS IF THE FRUIT OF SYSTEMIC
OPPRESSION IS SURPRISING.

AND THAT
APATHY
IS THE ANTITHESIS
OF UNCONDITIONAL LOVE.

INSTEAD, OUR
EMOTIONAL
RESPONSE
WILL BE MARKED BY
EMPATHY & COMPASSION,

REMEMBERING THAT
INACTION &
PASSIVITY
ARE DETRIMENTAL
TO JUSTICE,

LEADING TO A
REJECTION OF
PERFORMATIVE
ALLYSHIP
IN EXCHANGE FOR
THE REAL, VIGOROUS WORK.

AND, SHOULD
GUILT &
FATIGUE
TRY TO SETTLE IN,
WE'LL RECENTER THE NEEDS
OF THOSE YEARNING FOR LIBERATION,

The Cycle of Inaction

On January 6, 2021, I remember sobbing on the phone with my mom while watching insurrectionists storm the United States Capitol.

I wasn't shocked. I was tired.

I couldn't form many thoughts or find many words to describe how it all affected me, a then-25-year-old Black woman living in America. At that moment, I was experiencing a unique sense of frustration, not just because we as a nation are consistently finding ourselves reeling from blow after blow of injustice, but because it seems like, after each instance, we go in circles.

There's an outcry on social media, the story is front and center on the news cycle, brands and corporations make grand gestures of solidarity . . . and then, nothing. We move on and forget—until it happens again. And after a year of George Floyds, Breonna Taylors, and Ahmaud Arberys, the cycle was starting to take its toll on me.

The next day, on January 7, I began to write down what this cycle of injustices against the Black community felt like and named it the Cycle of Inaction. It starts when a horrific injustice takes place. Then there's widespread shock and confusion, as though we're unaware—or we've forgotten—that we're dealing with the fruit of seeds planted in racism and hatred. And then, whether triggered by pressure online or witnessing the distress of our neighbors, we have an emotional response ranging from anger to empathy to devil's advocacy, and as a result, many of us tumble into performative allyship, posting the posts and saying we're "doing the work," when in reality, many of us aren't doing much of anything. So guilt and fatigue show up, leading to inaction passivity, and resulting in apathy.

We know the world is fallen and broken. Instead of shocking us, it should serve as a constant reminder that we must always be ready to do the hard and holy things—not just with our words, thoughts, or social media posts, but with deeds: self-education, empathy, and choosing to lock arms instead of throwing fists. It's when we live into this posture that we know we'll always be ready to spring into action—not only when evil shows up again, but every day in between.

TAKE WHAT YOU NEED

A Time to Heal

Injustice is a thief. It robs its victims of peace, freedom, and safety. It also has physical consequences—it's exhausting, heavy, and draining. These very real implications make our battle against it twofold: while seeking to protect others from it, we must also protect ourselves. Below are a few ways to make space for healing in your heart as you continue on this journey.

Meditative Practices

Prayer, meditation, affirmations, breathwork—these and more are ways to ground yourself, rejuvenate your faith, and return to your center. Focusing on what is true, staying present, and leaning into spiritual practices can assist with reducing stress, anxiety, and exhaustion. You are worthy of peace in your mind and soul.

Connection

Connection is more than just a cure for the lonely. Together, we create space to process through hardship. We see and hear each other. Closeness fosters safety and familiarity—a place to retreat when we get weary. Building connection with others builds a sanctuary.

Enjoyment

You deserve joy. There's a quiet peace that comes over our hearts when we engage in the activities and practices that fill us with happiness and pleasure. You can have hobbies that are kept secret—ones that never make it to your social media feeds or small business storefronts. Lean into unmonetized, uncomplicated enjoyment and find healing there.

Rest

Whether it's a good night's sleep, a nap in the sunlight, or uninterrupted quiet time, let rest find you. Let your heart rate slow down and let your voicemail fill up. Surrender the need to fill every moment with work and lean into the reality that one way or another, it won't be complete. Be reminded of your tenderness and your humanity.

Create space to wander in search of what heals you. As you discover it, hold it close and let it guide you.

Everyone, Everywhere

It's tempting to believe that meaningful change isn't possible. With nearly eight billion people on the planet and a never-ending list of unmet needs, it's not unusual to question your own impact. Can we really achieve freedom and liberation for everyone, everywhere?

This reality could easily paint a picture of disappointment—but what if we viewed it as an invitation instead? Yes, perhaps the state of our world does hinder the possibility of freedom in totality. But instead of rendering you hopeless, let this reality remind you that there will always be someone, somewhere, who needs you and all of the good you give. Every tear in the tapestry of justice will need a mender. Each leg in the marathon for freedom will need a rested and ready runner to sub in for the weary and worn.

There are people in your orbit whom others will never meet. Each day, you're surrounded by a unique set of individuals, each with their own set of challenges and setbacks. Is anyone near you suffering? Is anyone struggling to be seen or heard? These moments matter. This is your assignment.

While it's critical to target overarching systems of harm and injustice, it's also necessary to lean into the opportunities currently surrounding you. You are needed right here, where you're planted—your home, your friend group, your neighborhood, your city. What you do here and now will determine the mark you leave on the world.

You've been invited. A special opportunity is knocking at your heart's door. Don't let pessimism rob you of the truth that liberation, no matter how elusive, should be available to anyone, anywhere. And any step toward that end is a step worth taking.

MICROAGGRESSIVE GREETING CARDS

Death by a Thousand Cuts

In the grand scheme of things, the fight for justice is more systemic than it is personal. Yet the focus on structural injustices doesn't absolve each of us from our own internal work weeding out racism, prejudice, and bias. In the same way that many small and positive actions can make a difference in the long run, many small and negative actions can add up over time with unfortunate consequences.

Psychologists who've observed those who live with the effects of bias, microaggressions, and stereotypes over time often describe the impact as "death by a thousand cuts," referring to the long-term effect of these practices on mental, physical, and emotional health. These sneaky slights and insults begin as thoughts and belief systems that often go ignored in the mind of the everyday person—and it's here where the work must begin.

Implicit bias can be hard to detect because we're often unaware of it. It's a set of unintentional thoughts and attitudes that inform our beliefs and actions toward certain groups of people, and we must work to both identify and weed them out. Microaggressions are often the result of implicit bias—they're everyday comments and behaviors that, although sometimes unintentional, demonstrate prejudice and come off as insulting or demeaning. They also play into stereotypes, the huge generalizations we make about whole groups of people—often historically excluded communities.

We do the work of ending the daily attacks on these communities by actively listening and adjusting our behavior when presented with new information. We don't look at a person and see them as a representative of their whole culture, but as a unique individual with a lived experience that extends far beyond our perceived understanding. When someone expresses their offense at your words or actions, believe them, and never see yourself as someone who's beyond learning.

PR VILEG

ILLUMINATED CAN

POINT S

TO HOW WE CAN

POUR OUT

FOR OTHERS

The Responsibility of Privilege

Privilege takes many forms, all of which are tied to those attributes that grant someone a higher status or standing in society than someone else. Chances are, you didn't ask for this. It's most likely innate or built in. Regardless, recognizing that we have them and becoming knowledgeable on how to use them can transform them into some of our greatest tools for change.

If you were to sit and take inventory of your life today, you'd most likely be able to identify many of the ways that you live with certain advantages. Perhaps you were born in the country you currently reside in and have never experienced the immigration process, or you come from a wealthy family and you've never had to stand in line at a community food bank. In some ways, privilege acts like a bunker—reducing exposure to certain difficulties and shielding us from experiencing certain hardships. Yet the goal is never to hide away as others experience marginalization and exclusion. We are called to get in the trenches.

Awakening to our own privileges in society should illuminate similar responsibilities. These benefits granted to us by our race, gender, sexuality, class, wealth, education, and more should lead us to come alive to the ways we can stand in the gap for those who suffer on the basis of these same identities. We can live a life poured out in pursuit of fairness and equity for the historically excluded among us, and one day, tear down the systems that are the source of this suffering.

Naming privilege is not an indictment. It does not erase any hardships or difficulties you've had to endure. It simply opens your eyes to the many ways you can uplift and amplify the crushed and mistreated. Together, we'll link the privileges we've been afforded to the responsibilities that go along with them as we work to make the world better for us all.

When Change Is Slow

There is no sting quite like that of defeat. We can plan, pray, and protest, but ultimately, much of what happens in life often feels out of our control. Disappointment with the way of the world isn't like that of losing a video game or placing last in a race. This grief can seep into our bones—exhausting us and tempting us with the notion that change cannot happen here.

Many will move on from choosing a life of good work, but many of us remain. If we want to continue this journey in any capacity, we must reckon with the weight of setbacks and interrupted plans. A different kind of plan must form—not one that details how to work our way to a win, but one that prepares us for lying down with losses. One that reminds us that although things haven't been changing in the ways we thought they would, that doesn't mean things aren't changing.

How do we prepare for those inevitable moments of defeat? Firstly, we must make room for grace. There is space to not have perfect outcomes, and any amount of good we put out is full of meaning and significance. Secondly, we must grieve. Processing and releasing what was lost creates space. Your disappointment matters—it's the evidence of your desire to see real change. It is worthy of being held.

Lastly, we hold on to hope. This can be fueled by looking back at those who came before us and seeing what pulled them through. Hope also drives our work toward progress. We may not always have a lot of it, but when planted and watered with reimagination, we remind ourselves that better is still to come. Light always finds a way to pierce through the darkest nights.

EQUITY VS. EQUALITY

EQUALITY

SAME AMOUNT OF PAINT GIVEN TO EACH ARTIST TO FILL THEIR OWN CANVAS, REGARDLESS OF SIZE

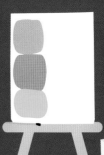

TASK COMPLETED WITH SOME PAINT LEFT OVER

JUST ENOUGH PAINT TO ADEQUATELY GET THE JOB DONE

NOT ENOUGH PAINT TO COMPLETE THE TASK

SAME RESOURCES, UNEQUAL OUTCOMES

EQUITY

ENOUGH PAINT GIVEN TO EACH ARTIST TO COMPLETELY FILL THEIR OWN CANVAS BASED ON ITS SIZE

A SMALL AMOUNT OF PAINT

A MEDIUM AMOUNT OF PAINT

A LARGE AMOUNT OF PAINT

PROPORTIONATE RESOURCES, EQUAL OUTCOMES

Equity's Full Picture

Envision a room with three artists, each given canvases of different sizes but the same amount of paint. Their only task is to fill their canvas with color. After painting for a while, Artist 1 finishes their piece with paint to spare. Artist 2 finishes soon after, with just enough paint to do the job. Artist 3 eventually runs out of paint after having only completed half of their piece.

What went wrong? Each artist was given the same amount of paint, but not all of them were able to complete the task because of the differing canvas sizes. This example illustrates how equality sometimes falls short. A group of people can all be given the same amount of resources yet have different needs. In society, this plays out in education, housing, workplaces, and countless other scenarios. Due to imbalances of power, discrimination, and systemic factors, many communities have greater needs and require more resources than others.

Equity seeks to paint the full picture. An equitable solution involves resources being given proportionately and resulting in equal outcomes, or all needs being met. In the scenario of the three artists, equity would involve not merely providing the same amount of paint, but giving enough paint to each artist so they can fill each canvas according to its size.

Justice work recognizes that equal resources won't always result in equal outcomes. The goal of equity is to fill in those gaps, personalizing our good work to support all people according to their needs. It's an opportunity to get creative with how we spark change—not through a one-size-fits-all approach, but through recognizing that the end goal is to fill in all the blanks until the full picture is complete.

Diversity Is the Fruit

I'm no stranger to predominantly white spaces. Growing up in a town where we were one of a few Black families, I often expected to be the only Black girl in the room. When I entered my profession after college, I largely operated under a diversity-focused mindset. I believed that if we just got more people of color in predominantly white spaces, it would solve a lot of race-related issues in organizations I found myself a part of.

Instead, I noticed an even bigger issue: the focus on diversity was largely performative. Members of historically excluded communities would join a team, church, or social circle to find themselves still faced with the same discrimination, exclusion, and discomfort they had grown accustomed to. We see this same diversity-focused harm in many areas of life—Black and brown bodies used for metrics but not infused into a culture of true belonging.

When diversity is forced without true structural change to back it up, the efforts largely fall flat. In order for true change to take place, the focus has to shift from a diversity-focused mindset of "getting more people of color in here" to an equity-focused mindset of "how can we change our current processes and remove barriers to allow for diversity—in all forms—to flourish here."

When we adopt an equity-focused mindset, we attack imbalances at the root and pave the way to inclusion and belonging, creating an equitable space where all people truly feel welcome, heard, and protected.

And in an environment like that, diversity has room to bloom.

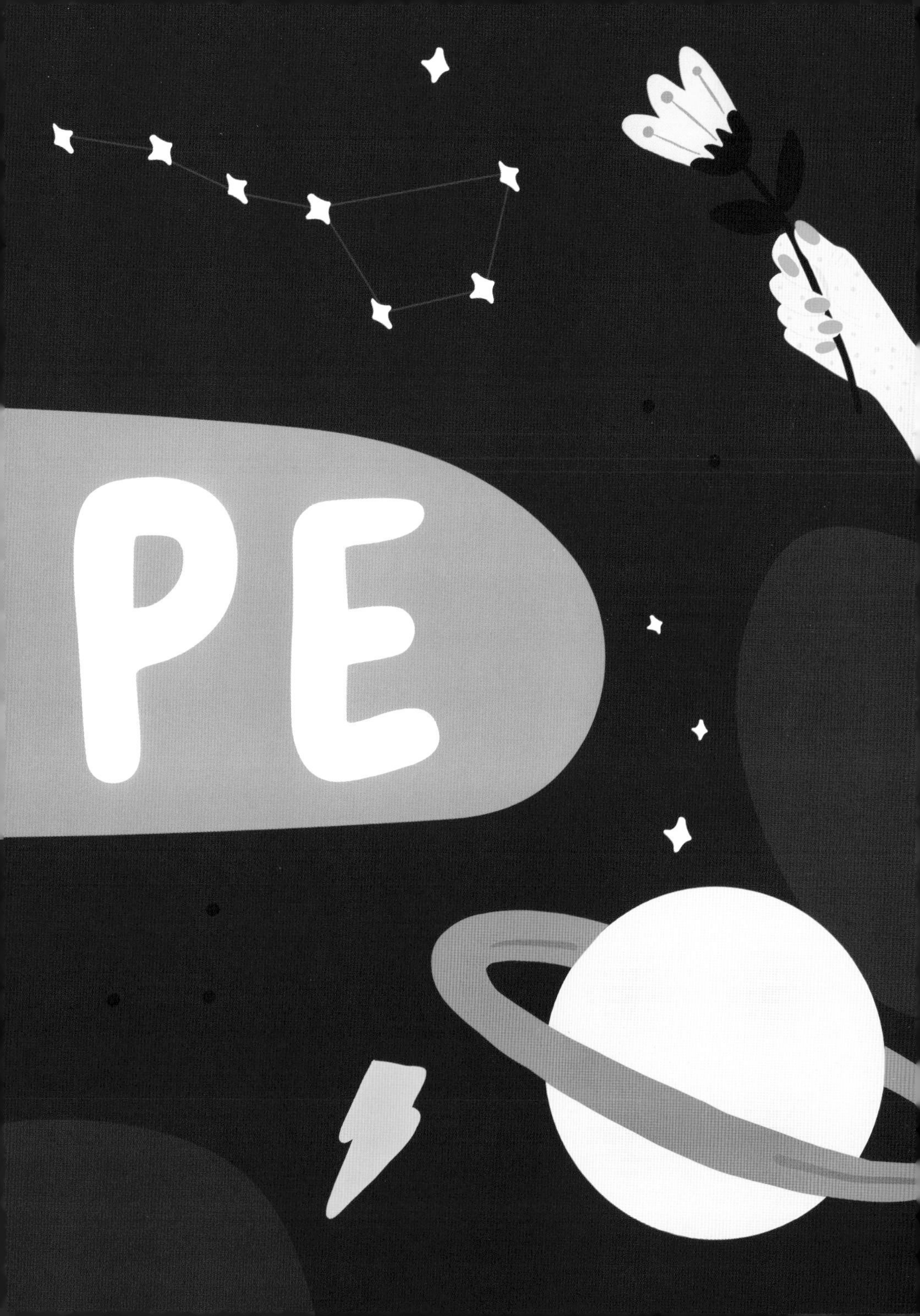
PE

ON HOPE, I BUILD A FOUNDATION.

WITH HOPE, I LIVE IN EXPECTATION.

IN HOPE, I FIND RESTORATION.

Hope Through Life's Journey

On hope, I build a foundation.

I ground myself in the belief that what's to come will be better than what's behind me. With hope as my foundation, I am consistently reoriented to a hopeful disposition. When circumstances lead me to despair and doubt, I allow myself to be recentered by my confidence that this won't be the end of me. I manually change my default setting to everlasting hope.

With hope, I live in expectation.

I anticipate that beautiful, good things will happen. I am always looking for the cracks where the light pours in. I don't just move through time wishing that evil won't thwart my best-laid plans: I factor in the possibility and still resolve that evil will not rule the day. I move with confident inertia, intent on continual forward movement until an outside force acts upon me—and, even then—I will continue on afterward, ever moving forward.

In hope, I find rest.

When I'm overcome with weariness and stress, I take a break from my worrying and make my bed in hope. I allow hope to rescue me from my desolation and gently lift my head toward a future filled with possibility. I gaze beyond the valley of my current situation and look up toward the mountains and hills—reminders that the journey does not end here in this low valley. I give my mind a break from constantly thinking through worst-case scenarios and allow hope to remind me, "This will not be the end of you."

ALLOW YOURSELF TO
GRIEVE WHAT WAS LOST,
WHAT YOU THOUGHT WOULD CHANGE, AND
WHAT REMAINS OF YOUR UNMET EXPECTATIONS.
PROCESS AND RELEASE THE WEIGHT OF
DISAPPOINTMENT OVER THE CURRENT
STATE OF THINGS. AND MAYBE, IN THE
SPACE ONCE OCCUPIED BY THE HEAVINESS
OF WHAT COULD HAVE BEEN, YOU CAN
PLANT A SEED OF HOPE AS YOU
REIMAGINE WHAT COULD BE.

The Tension of Hope

To yearn for anything is to put your heart at risk. Our deepest longings—for belonging, community, justice, peace—are often met with resistance. We are no strangers to disappointment. We can recount the moments when the relationship failed, the deal fell through, or the "no" knocked on our front door.

Encountering disappointment on your journey often leads you to a fork in the road. You're faced with two main decisions: Will you continue on this journey with hope, or will you veer off the path and become detoured by pessimism? Neither path will be easy, but one is sure to sidetrack you and stunt your growth.

We must balance the recognition of disappointment with the belief that although this did not work out, greater is still possible. Instead of shoving down our true emotions and hurriedly turning the page to the next chapter, we can hold the tension of hope: it has not happened for me yet, but I've seen it happen before, and I believe it will happen again. Even if the future does not turn out the way we desire, hope has a way of reminding us that good things have a way of finding us one way or another.

Allow yourself to grieve what was lost, what you thought would change, and what remains of your unmet expectations. Process and release the weight of disappointment over the current state of things. And maybe, in the space once occupied by the heaviness of what could have been, you can plant a seed of hope as you reimagine what could be.

SOMETIMES WE NEED TO LOOK

BACKWARD

TO FORGE A BETTER PATH

FORWARD

The Windshield and Rearview

The road of hope winds and bends. We set out with our hearts' particular destinations, anticipating our arrivals with a sense of deep longing—but when the way and the waiting seem long, it's easy to be lured away by fear and doubt.

While it may feel like the only constant is your unchanging circumstance, remember that you are surrounded by reminders. Look around you—allow the rearview mirror of your mind to take you back to the prayers answered, dreams actualized, and wishes granted. You leave a trail of miracles behind you.

The windshield is bigger than the rearview mirror on purpose. Before you lie endless possibilities: the curiosities of roads not yet traveled, distant mountain ranges of mystery, and dark forests waiting to foil your best-laid plans. What's ahead of you should take up the bulk of your attention. Yet the rearview, however small, also serves a beautiful purpose.

Your past is always trying to tell you something. It may whisper lies of shame or regret, making you cringe at memories of trauma or stinging with the pain of grief. On the other hand, your past can be proof of your progress. It can remind you of the ways you've overcome and equip you with the ability to recognize danger. It can fill you with joy and pride as you recount the ways you've weathered the storms, emerging fortified. Your past can inform your future, passing along the intel you gained through your encounters and experiences.

There's no telling what's ahead for you, but as you seek out the desires of your heart, be reminded that you already have many victories under your belt. You have hiked steep paths before. Look ahead—and when you reach your next mountaintop, look back to guide others with the stories of how you made it through.

WHAT HISTORY TEACHES US

- THINGS WE SHOULD NEVER DO AGAIN!
- where we went wrong
- THE ORIGIN OF OPPRESSION
- THE CONSEQUENCES OF OUR ACTIONS

WHAT HISTORY ALSO TEACHES US

- HOPE IS AN ANCHOR
- THE POWER OF PERSEVERANCE
- change is possible
- OUR GOOD WORK MATTERS
- no one can STEAL OUR JOY!

Hope and Memory

Comfort can be found in recollection. Looking back on how far you've come is encouraging, but it's also helpful to look back at those who've come before you. Who are your heroes? Who blazed the trail of progress for the causes that matter most to you? Sitting with the struggles, triumphs, thoughts, and works of those who paved the way can unlock a sense of hope and inspiration for the journey ahead.

One reality you may notice upon looking back is that others faced familiar obstacles. The leaders we look up to had their share of trials, many of which have shown up in society today in different ways. The heroes of the Civil Rights Movement wrestled with injustice at a systemic level, battled for voting rights, and experienced lukewarm participation in the cause from bystanders and onlookers. While these issues have changed form in modern-day society, we can learn from the tactics and mindsets of those who've fought these fights before us and find hope in the fact that they achieved progress.

Another comforting relief we discover in the search through memory is the existence of familiar kinds of people. We find humans, just like us, who wrestled with similar flaws or vices. We also find people who made tremendous strides toward progress while being the target of unjust laws and policies. While we wish that they didn't have to bear the weight of oppression and marginalization, we're reminded that change is possible and that we can be the ones who make change happen.

Purpose can be found in the losses and the wins. When we peel back the curtain of memory and search through time, we'll be constantly reminded of how our efforts matter, how injustice can be thwarted, and how our shortcomings don't disqualify us from being valuable participants in a life of good work.

HOPEFUL
FOR THE
PROGRESS
AND GROWTH
THAT'S TO
COME

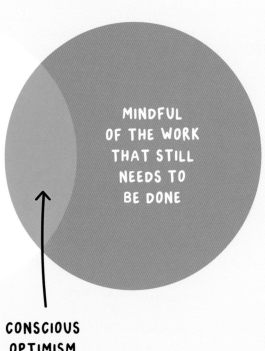

MINDFUL
OF THE WORK
THAT STILL
NEEDS TO
BE DONE

CONSCIOUS
OPTIMISM

Conscious Optimism

After the 2020 election wrapped up, I saw a particular phrase swirling around on the internet. The phrase was "cautious optimism," and it filled me with curiosity. Is this the kind of hope I wanted to move forward with?

Don't get me wrong, the idea made complete sense to me. After a season of heightened division, uncertainty, sickness, and state-sanctioned violence, there was safety in the idea of carefully and slowly moving toward the flickering light of hope that we strained our eyes to see in the distance. Running toward hope seemed to be a dangerous set-up for discouragement, and with no idea what was truly on the horizon, wisdom whispered: "Slow and steady." Even so, the "cautious" label didn't seem to be the right fit for me.

You see, my definition of hope is simply that what's to come will be greater than what's behind. While it sounds idealistic, it actually comes with a level of responsibility. We don't arrive at "greater" through wishful thinking, or even cautiously tiptoeing toward the future. "Greater" takes effort, strategy, and a healthy dose of realism—the humbling reminder that we can't solve everything, but we do have the power to solve something.

Healthy realism combined with an awareness of the work we need to do helped me land at "conscious" optimism. To be conscious is to be awake, perceiving the world around you with eyes wide open. Conscious optimism says that while we're hopeful for the progress and growth that's to come, we're also mindful of the work that still needs to be done, and we hold both truths with equal weight. It's in this delicate balance of future yearning and present actuality that we become equipped, in both heart and mind, to continue running the race set before us—knowing that endurance is what brings hope down to earth.

THEY FOLLOWED THE STARS

SO WE COULD FOLLOW OUR DREAMS

The Hope of Our Ancestors

There's much to be said about drawing from memory to find hope, yet there's another aspect of hope and history that is futuristic in nature. As I look back, I'm reminded of how my ancestors *looked forward*.

When we trace the lineage of the African diaspora, we find enslaved people who chased stars through the darkness to find freedom. They sang of a future of liberation with the hope that they'd live to see it, with lyrics like "I ain't got long to stay here" hinting at the belief that trouble wouldn't last always. Black activists and preachers echoed these sentiments in the mid-1900s, with leaders like Dr. Martin Luther King Jr. sharing dreams of a future where his children weren't bound up by racism and could finally be free.

It seems that my ancestors' efforts were fueled by the hope that the future was bright and full of freedom. Even enslaved people, who knew mostly sorrow and had little-to-no evidence that better was possible, clung to this hope. Today, we have become the evidence. How much more should we—people who have tasted and seen the fruit of this hope—continue to believe that good is still on the horizon?

Even when we cannot see, something within us yearns for freedom and moves toward hope. We are our ancestors' wishes come to fruition. Let this hope push you to shoot for the moon, for they followed the stars so we could follow our dreams.

TEN TRUTHS TO CLING TO

MY CURRENT CIRCUMSTANCE—AND ITS LEVEL OF SEVERITY—IS TEMPORARY IN NATURE. ONE DAY, I WILL LOOK BACK AND SEE THAT I HAVE EITHER PASSED THROUGH IT OR GROWN AROUND IT.

HAVING HOPE IS NOT DENYING MY PRESENT SITUATION, BUT RESOLVING THAT THIS IS NOT THE END OF MY STORY.

I HAVE WITNESSED THE POWER OF PERSEVERANCE AND HAVE SEEN TRANSFORMATION SPRING FORTH FROM THE MOST UNLIKELY PLACES.

I AM NOT ALONE IN MY SUFFERING AND THERE ARE PEOPLE WHO LOVE ME AND WANT TO WALK WITH ME THROUGH THIS SEASON.

MY HOPE STRENGTHENS MY ABILITY TO ENDURE. MY BELIEF THAT GREATER THINGS ARE COMING GIVES ME THE POWER TO MOVE FORWARD.

WHEN HOPE FEELS DISTANT

DWINDLED HOPE DOES NOT EQUATE TO A LACK OF FAITH. DOUBT AND BELIEF ARE NOT ENEMIES. I AM WORTHY, EVEN IN THE MIDST OF MY UNCERTAINTY.

MY GRIEF AND SORROW ARE WELCOME. I AM NOT A BOTHER. I AM FREE TO EXIST IN MY CURRENT REALITY WITHOUT SHAME.

I CAN FIND BEAUTY IN MY WAITING. I DON'T HAVE TO SEE THE FINISH LINE TO FIND JOY IN MY JOURNEY.

SOME OF THE MOST IMPACTFUL CHANGEMAKERS HAVE WRESTLED WITH HOPELESSNESS. MY IMPACT DOES NOT DECREASE IN VALUE WHEN MY HOPE STARTS TO FADE.

I BELIEVE THAT GOOD HAS A WAY OF CONQUERING EVIL IN THE END. SORROW WILL NOT HAVE THE FINAL SAY.

WHEN THE BRIGHT SIDE GETS TOO BRIGHT

COMMON PHRASES ASSOCIATED WITH TOXIC POSITIVITY

When Positivity Gets Dangerous

As a generally optimistic person with a hopeful disposition, I'm used to seeing the glass as half-full. I'm the textbook definition of an Enneagram Type Seven. For years, I tried to avoid all negative emotions at any cost, leading to the cultivation of poor habits like stifling my true feelings and having difficulty with processing pain. Looking back, what I thought was a cheery outlook on life turned out to be the symptoms of toxic positivity.

Toxic positivity is the die-hard dedication to happy thoughts, even when inappropriate. Those who succumb to it often forsake the necessity of sitting with and processing through tough emotions for the alluring facade of "good vibes only." Not only can this be detrimental to your own well-being, but it can also inhibit your ability to support others in their times of need.

When trying to encourage someone, I envision toxic positivity as shining a bright flashlight directly into someone else's eyes. With every "Just look on the bright side!" and "Only think happy thoughts," you overwhelm them with rays of good intentions while overlooking their need to process and grieve in their own timing. When someone is sitting in the dark, shining a light directly into their eyes does nothing to repair their inability to see hope in the world around them.

This doesn't mean that there's no room for hopeful encouragement—it's simply a reminder that our actions should be more intentional than invasive. Imagine that this flashlight of positivity is replaced with a candle of hope, one for you and one for your neighbor. Your candle may be burning brightly in this season, and theirs may not be. What a beautiful opportunity to turn to them and say, "At this moment, I have enough hope for the both of us . . . and when you're ready, I'll light your candle too."

THINGS TO REMEMBER
ABOUT STORMS

THEY CAUSE US
TO SLOW DOWN

THEY CAN BE
SCARY AND
CHAOTIC

THEY WON'T
LAST FOREVER

THEY HELP
THINGS GROW

Things to Remember about Storms

A storm is a destructive mystery. Sometimes, we see it coming and can brace for impact. Other times, it catches us by surprise, knocking the wind out of us and leaving rubble in its wake. While difficult to wait through, there are things to remember about storms that can bring a sense of comfort or peace:

They can be scary and chaotic.
This specific fact isn't very comforting or peaceful, but it does give us permission to name and acknowledge how hard things can be. It's tempting to look past difficulty and shove down the reality of a situation, never really experiencing the relief that can come from feeling your feelings and letting them pass through. Acknowledging this can remind you that it's okay to recognize the difficulty of something, and letting it run its course can be freeing in the end.

They cause us to slow down.
Storms remind us that some things truly aren't as urgent as we once believed. Hardships often stop us in our tracks, making us clear out our calendars or put things on hold. Rest and healing can be found in a reduced pace.

They help things grow.
Life's difficulties have a way of fortifying our character and reminding us of what's truly valuable in this life. To be clear, you are a person, not a self-improvement project—storms don't exist to continuously make you a better person. They simply exist, and the changes we experience in our lives are the aftermath. We often come out on the other side softer, gentler, and more empathetic people.

They won't last forever.
Tough circumstances are not permanent. While the pain of loss, failure, or grief may live long, we have the capacity to exist and grow around them until they are present without completely overtaking us.

Storms do not have to be the end of your story. When you don't know what your next steps should be, remind yourself that you can make it through this, and you will one day encourage others with the person you've become on the other side of this destruction.

TENDING TO THE GARDEN OF YOUR DREAMS

STEPS TO TAKE AS YOU HOPE FOR HARVEST

CUT AWAY
THE DOUBTS
THAT CLAIM
YOU'RE UNABLE
TO SUCCEED

GET PLANTED IN
CONFIDENCE AND
BELIEF

SOIL

NOURISH YOUR
MIND WITH
INSPIRATION
AND FRESH
IDEAS

DIG OUT
FEELINGS OF
UNWORTHINESS
OR IMPOSTER
SYNDROME

GIVE YOURSELF
ROOM TO BLOOM
AND GROW

Hope for the Harvest

My dad is a self-taught farmer. Year after year, he plants seeds of all kinds in his backyard garden, carefully tending to them each day. From mini greenhouses and heating contraptions to homemade trenches and fertilizer, he dedicates himself to giving his various plants the attention they need to thrive. At the end of the day, farmers don't just plant things for the fun of it, but to one day see the literal fruit of their labor. They hope, wait for, and work toward a harvest. As we plant and till the soil of our own lives, there are lessons to be found in our own waiting to see our dreams come to pass.

The first step to reaping the harvest of our efforts is to adequately prepare. Whether you're wanting to start a small business, build a nonprofit, or move to a new city, harvest is predicated on our ability to make room for it. We make sure that we're creating environments that foster growth—in our own lives, as well as the lives of those we seek to impact. This also involves gaining knowledge, grabbing supplies, and taking inventory of the personal efforts and sacrifices that will be needed to bring this dream to life.

We must also be willing to take daily steps to tend to the growth of our dreams. As the farmer spends each day watering, tilling, and pruning, so must we take steps to foster our own progress. It's here where we're reminded that growth doesn't happen overnight, and a consistent dedication over time is what helps us make it happen. Even when we don't see progress, we can draw strength from our hope and use our desire for harvest as a source of inspiration.

In our hopes to see positive change in our world, we also see the realities of what it takes to get there. All of the planning and preparation in the world can't prevent tragedy and disaster from wiping out our efforts. Even then, we know that seasons change, and our steady work toward the harvest is fueled by our radical and unwavering hope that the harvest will come.

ALL ABOUT
THAT TOPIC!

A WAR

APPROACHING CONVERSATIONS WITH AN
OPEN MIND AND NUANCED PERSPECTIVES

AWAKENING TO OUR OWN
TENDENCIES TO CAUSE HARM

BECOMING MORE AWARE OF
INJUSTICES AROUND US

BEING INSPIRED TO
ACT DIFFERENTLY

THE EVIDENCE OF A CHANGED PERSPECTIVE

SEEING THE WORLD THROUGH NEW EYES

Eyes Wide Open

Discovery is a natural part of our life from birth. Picture the wonder of an infant: eyes open wide as they look at the world around them, seeing everything for the very first time. We feel that sense of awe with every exciting new experience, and those memories often stick with us.

When it comes to the state of our society, many of us can remember our first "eyes wide open" moment—the statement, incident, or epiphany that jolted us from ignorance to awareness. For many who joined the Black Lives Matter movement in 2020, that moment was the murder of George Floyd. For those passionate about ending gun violence, the Parkland mass shooting may have triggered their lightbulb moment. Whatever the cause, the sudden shift in perspective is a crucial starting point for those who decide to dedicate their lives to change-making.

The difference between those who will take action and those who will remain passive lies in what happens after the switch flips on. To become aware of the injustices around you is to see the world with a fresh pair of eyes. Take note: what can you now see that's been there all along? How does this realization feel in your mind, heart, and throughout your body? What do you feel called to do next?

Now that you're aware, you have been assigned a new sense of responsibility. Your newfound knowledge now requires something of you. You could choose to retreat back to your old patterns of living, willfully ignorant of the part you play in the improvement of our society—or you could bravely embark on a new journey full of learning, growth, and discovery. We'll always be invited to adopt fresh perspectives. Choosing to live your life with eyes wide open makes all the difference.

PAY ATTENTION TO
CURRENT ISSUES
AND LISTEN TO
VOICES THAT ARE
OFTEN SILENCED

LEAN INTO
THEIR UNIQUE
CHANGEMAKING
ROLE AND USE
THEIR GIFTS
FOR PROGRESS

CONSISTENTLY
TAKE INVENTORY
OF THEIR OWN
BIASES AND
PRIVILEGES

CHARACTERISTICS OF EVERYDAY ADVOCATES

SPEND TIME
LEARNING ABOUT
CAUSES AND WAYS
TO CONTRIBUTE

SPREAD
AWARENESS
ABOUT THE
IMPORTANCE
OF ISSUES

We Won't All Be Activists

Protests, boycotts, and other types of public demonstrations are commonly tied to progress. Across a wide range of issues, activism helps society move from wishful thinking to tangible transformation with real-life consequences. While an important part of changemaking, many of us won't find ourselves joining marches and protests that often—yet all of us are still valuable participants in the push for progress.

Many dictionaries define activism as vigorous action for social or political change. There is much to be said about the word "vigorous." It's a demanding word. It's intense, unrelenting, and forceful. To be an activist is to consistently be doing the intense work of being on the frontlines of change, often putting your body on the line for the good of a cause.

You may be reading this and surveying your own life—thinking about your job, family, caretaking responsibilities, or personal difficulties, and wondering if there's a place for you in this kind of work. Rest assured—there's a place for you, even if it's not on the frontlines.

The beauty of moving forward is that it always takes multiple roles to get us there. We will need teachers, artists, listeners, empaths, learners, encouragers, truth-tellers, planners, cheerleaders, and so much more on the many paths to progress. We won't all be activists, and that's beautiful news.

There will be moments where your frontlines will be your family, your inner work, and your personal well-being. Your capacity won't always allow for vigorous action. Even still, be reminded that your role is more valuable than you could ever imagine, and there's always room for what you're able to bring—even if it doesn't look the way you think it should.

	HIGH CONTEXT	**LOW CONTEXT**
← CONTEXT →		
HIGH CAPACITY	THE EDUCATOR	THE LEARNER
LOW CAPACITY	THE ADVOCATE	THE AMPLIFIER

FINDING OUR STARTING ROLES

CHANGEMAKING RELATIVE TO OUR CONTEXT AND CAPACITY

Finding Your Starting Role

When exposed to a new cause or opportunity to make a difference, it's common to feel completely lost, not knowing where to start or what to do first. This often happens most when tragedy strikes in our country or the world at large—issues feel so big that it's hard to find our place in the solution.

Inspired by the Eisenhower Decision Matrix, the "Finding Your Starting Role" framework serves to help you identify your next steps by weighing two crucial factors: your context and your capacity. Context doesn't just refer to the knowledge you have about a situation, but also your proximity to it based on your own lived experience. Capacity refers to the time, space, and ability you have to dedicate to a cause or issue.

If you have high context and high capacity with the issue at hand, you're needed on the frontlines of changemaking as an educator, mobilizing those around you. If you've got high capacity but not a lot of context, times of crisis may not be the best time to jump into educating others until you've done some of your own learning. That way, you're way more equipped to spread accurate information—not misinformation.

Being an advocate is helpful for others when you've got context and knowledge on a current issue but not much capacity to take on the role of an educator. Advocating can include recommending organizations to partner with or pointing people in the right direction with resources. If you don't have a lot of context or capacity to dive deep into resources, this is your opportunity to amplify the voices of those educating and advocating by listening, encouraging, or shining a light on what they're sharing.

These aren't firm rules but can be a great place to start if you want to make a difference from a place of honest self-reflection. When we let those with the most context and proximity to issues lead us, we find out how we can best lend a hand relative to our resources and abilities.

READING THE SIGNALS

SHOWIING SOLIDARITY WITH HISTORICALLY EXCLUDED COMMUNITIES

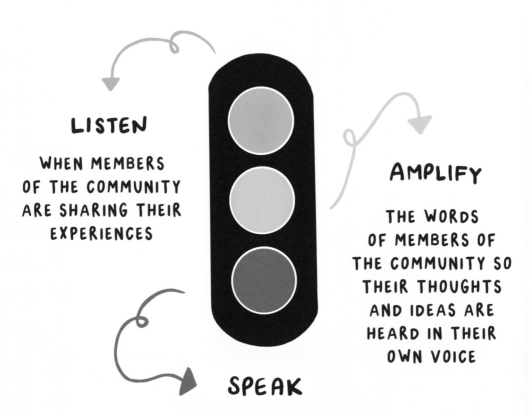

LISTEN

WHEN MEMBERS OF THE COMMUNITY ARE SHARING THEIR EXPERIENCES

AMPLIFY

THE WORDS OF MEMBERS OF THE COMMUNITY SO THEIR THOUGHTS AND IDEAS ARE HEARD IN THEIR OWN VOICE

SPEAK

WHEN YOU WITNESS INJUSTICE OR HAVE AN OPPORTUNITY TO ADVOCATE

Reading the Signals

When it comes to conversations involving the advancement of historically excluded communities, you'd be surprised how often those very same communities are talked over or left out. There is an art to making sure that those on the receiving end of injustice are properly heard, amplified, and given the platform to speak to what the needs are in a way that prioritizes dignity and equity.

Consider the traffic light—it sends signals for who goes and who waits. These same principles can apply to how we navigate conversations surrounding equity.

First, it's important to listen. Allow members of historically excluded communities to be heard without censoring, interruption, or silencing. As experiences are shared and perspectives are explained, those voices are prioritized and dignified. Members of these communities were never voiceless but have often been silenced.

Picture a person speaking at a normal volume, and then someone coming up beside them with a megaphone, holding it up to the speaking person's mouth to let the sound travel farther. That's amplifying—using what you have to help someone else's voice be heard. We are all experts of our own stories, and helping someone share their own story is liberating.

Listening and amplifying equips us to speak out in partnership with communities who desire true, meaningful change. Using our own voices allows us to stand in the gap for others, call out harm, and advocate for change. When we read the signals in conversations for progress, we make sure that suppressed voices are heard and amplified, while doing what we can to be part of the solution too.

SPEAK TO THE HEART OF IT!! 🖤🖤

Using Your Voice

Progress depends on the people who are willing to speak up. From calling out bigotry at the dinner table to protesting in the streets of our cities, change is activated by those who decide that staying silent is not an option. As someone who has spoken out against harm and injustice for years, both online and offline, I've learned many lessons and racked up nuggets of advice that have served me well in the work I do. Here are two that you may find helpful too:

Speak the truth of the matter.
Your efficacy hinges on your accuracy. Before you speak out about anything, take a moment to ensure that you know the facts and have consulted a few primary sources. Nothing damages the credibility of your voice quite like being inaccurate and spreading misinformation. When you do have the facts, don't beat around the bush. Speak the truth of the matter clearly, without clouding it with your desire to maintain a sense of peace. Not every medicinal truth can go down with a spoonful of sugar.

Speak to the heart of the matter.
This tactic is one that I practice religiously and one that often goes overlooked by the majority. While others are focusing on smaller, more supporting details that don't have a drastic effect on the main issue at hand, focus on the bottom line. Raise your head above the weeds of fruitless side narratives and distracting talking points until you're at eye-level with the heart of the matter—the important truth that needs to be taken away from the issue you're speaking out about. While details and subtopics do matter, it's easy to get so lost in the noise that the main message is missed. Keep your eyes on the target.

When using your voice, remember to be pointed, direct, and clear. Accurately define what's happening and identify the heart of the issue so that you're making the most impact with your words. The clearer the takeaway, the more applicable the lesson is to the lives of the people you seek to influence.

THINGS YOU CHOOSE NOT TO SEE
WHEN YOU CLAIM TO NOT SEE COLOR:

THE COMPLEXITIES OF RACIAL ISSUES

YOUR OWN BLIND SPOTS AND PREJUDICES

THE UNIQUE STRUGGLES OF BLACK
PEOPLE AND PEOPLE OF COLOR

INSTANCES OF RACIALIZED VIOLENCE

PART OF WHAT MAKES A PERSON
WHO THEY ARE AND AFFECTS HOW
THEY MOVE THROUGH SOCIETY

Seeing in Color

It was a bright, cheery morning when I sat at a table for two in a small coffee shop. I was full of hope as my boss sat across from me, waiting with a drink in hand to discuss what was on my mind for our hour-long meeting on diversity and inclusion in the workplace.

I began listing off examples of reasons why I thought we needed to focus on it as a team: from examples of casual racism among employees to my feelings of discomfort surrounding being the only Black woman in the company. I made my case with excitement and couldn't wait to dream about the future.

My boss looked at me and said a sentence that would change my life's trajectory from that very moment:

"Well, I don't see color."

I sat, dumbfounded and disappointed as he detailed why he wasn't passionate about this subject and how he couldn't see himself spending company money or time to do anything about it. How could someone who claimed to love me regardless of my race be so adamant about not working to improve my circumstances that were seemingly caused by it?

That's the problem with the "I don't see color" mentality—by claiming to not see race, you actually fail to see all the inequities and systemic injustices that come along with it. Adopting this mindset is, in essence, choosing to tap out of the work required to improve the conditions of those who have been victimized by racism.

Awareness involves opening our eyes to all that sets us apart. In embracing our unique cultures, backgrounds, and identities, we are better equipped to fight alongside those who've been historically marginalized and excluded, while also discovering how our own personal work of unpacking prejudice and racism should be addressed. We cannot be known until we are seen.

On Dignity

We are all worthy by nature. We were born with inherent value, each of us deserving of being treated with respect and decency. The concept of dignity reminds us that as human beings, we share a common baseline of worth—yet not everyone gets to experience this right.

Consider the unhoused, who often are so rejected in society that they rarely even experience eye contact, or the food donation centers consistently overrun with expired, unhealthy food. Recall the on-screen depictions of those living in nations battling poverty, or the countless stories of elder abuse in our nation's nursing homes. For many, experiencing dignity is a luxury.

It's also possible to forget the importance of dignity within our own relationships and day-to-day interactions. Picture someone being cut off while they speak, preventing them from sharing their own thoughts and beliefs; or another being deprived of the freedom to make their own choices. When boundaries aren't respected and rights are infringed upon, we rob people of their dignity.

Restoration happens when we prioritize the humanity and worth of each individual we come across. It's looking someone in the eye when they speak, or not impeding on their right to agency and decision-making. For those struggling with poverty, we dignify them by giving from our best, not our leftovers. Choosing dignity means rejecting stereotypes and protecting human rights, both locally and globally.

How can you remind someone of their value and worth today? See them. Look beyond their present circumstance or standing in society and choose their humanity. Love limitlessly, reach out to those who feel forgotten, and lift the heads of the lowly. We belong to each other.

LISTENING and LEARNING and SPEAKING and DOING

Picking a Cause

Have you ever had trouble narrowing down a cause to support? You're not alone. There are so many opportunities to make a difference in the world around you—so much so that getting specific can get a bit tricky. If you're searching for guidance, try looking in these three places: personal experiences, passions, and proximity.

It's not uncommon to support a cause that you have a personal connection to. Perhaps a family member has dealt with a difficult diagnosis, you've recently adopted an animal from a shelter, or you've had your own struggles with mental health. Personal experience is a powerful connector to causes that need support. Consider tapping into that well of personal experience and seeing what floats to the surface.

Another source of inspiration when choosing a cause is what you're already passionate about. Recall those moments when a particular news headline tugged at your heart, or a specific issue kept you up at night. What do you really care about? What makes your heart swell? Your passions can help steer you in the direction toward causes that you can support for a lifetime.

Some causes that we support won't always be the ones that jump out at us. Many will find us based on proximity—how close we are to the issue and how directly affected we are by its consequences. This is what often leads people to campaign for clean water in their city after months of waiting for relief, or to show up to a school board meeting when their students' rights to read are threatened in the classroom. Our closeness to an issue often informs our response to it.

Hopefully, your wheels are turning. No matter where you land, know that your efforts will never be in vain. Get specific, get local, and get out there.

NARROWING DOWN YOUR ACTION

FROM INFORMATION OVERLOAD TO PURPOSE – FUELED PROGRESS

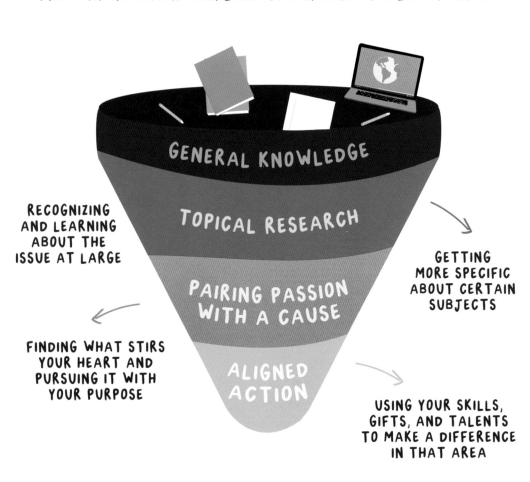

GENERAL KNOWLEDGE

TOPICAL RESEARCH

PAIRING PASSION WITH A CAUSE

ALIGNED ACTION

RECOGNIZING AND LEARNING ABOUT THE ISSUE AT LARGE

GETTING MORE SPECIFIC ABOUT CERTAIN SUBJECTS

FINDING WHAT STIRS YOUR HEART AND PURSUING IT WITH YOUR PURPOSE

USING YOUR SKILLS, GIFTS, AND TALENTS TO MAKE A DIFFERENCE IN THAT AREA

Narrowing Down Your Action

While experiencing a newfound awareness of a topic or cause, it's not unusual to want to do a deep dive into all there is to know about the subject. We'll do online searches, read books, follow educators, and watch documentaries until our heads almost explode with the newfound knowledge. This often leads to a conundrum known as information overload—a dilemma that can cause us to stop learning altogether because we're so overwhelmed.

Narrowing down your action helps you go from information overload to purpose-fueled progress. As long as we're alive, we'll be students of something. A framework for learning will help you pace yourself in your discoveries as you tend to the many other areas of your life that also need your attention.

Any learning process begins with the intake of general knowledge. This is the wide opening of your information-to-action funnel. Learn from any medium, focusing on reliable sources and strategies that compliment your desired ways of gaining information. These can be podcasts, videos, articles, and more—the choice is yours—but the ultimate goal is gaining a broad understanding of the topic at hand.

Next, hone in on specific aspects of the larger topic by conducting topical research. This is where you start to narrow down on parts of a topic that interest you the most or stir your heart in unique ways. From there, identify how you can connect your passions with one of those topics and eventually take aligned action: using your gifts and talents to leave a mark on your world through the knowledge you've gained from this topic.

Following this framework can lead you from gaining general knowledge about a subject to learning about its specific implications. The possibilities are endless, and attainable, when you turn your awareness into action in ways that are unique to you.

The Journey of Lifelong Learning

Choosing to live a life of awareness means assuming the role of a lifelong learner. It takes humility to confess that you will never truly "arrive," and that the journey is a collection of hills and valleys that test your commitment and teach you transformative lessons. As you make the climb, remember that the bumps along the way are completely normal and to be expected. The strides of your successes are larger than the ones of your mistakes.

Prepare yourself to consistently receive and apply new information. While you won't internalize everything you learn, remember that progress is ever evolving, and your flexibility will become a tool for consistently moving forward. You'll find yourself in a continuous state of studying, growing, and changing perspectives, expanding your capacity for change and your empathy for others.

As much as you're learning, you'll also be unlearning. The harmful ideologies and practices you've picked up in life will need to be put down to make room in your hands for your growth. This unlearning will sometimes take the form of being held accountable and getting called in, but when done with good intentions, this healthy accountability will feel like a pruning process. The old, unhealthy parts of you will be cut away to prevent your growth from being stunted.

You're not alone on this journey. In those moments when you pause to catch your breath, you'll look up and see that your neighbors are walking similar paths, doing the best they can right alongside you. Cling to your community and make your path to progress a group effort. Be open to failing forward. To be a perpetual student of life is to honor that we are always growing and that the path won't be linear, but as long as you're willing, you're sure to be embarking on the adventure of a lifetime.

COMM

UNITY

Collective Liberation

Although we are individuals, we do not exist independently of each other. One person's actions may be another person's consequences. We crave community by default, and even the most introverted among us have deep desires for belonging.

No one wins in an oppressive society. Consider a dystopia like Gilead in Margaret Atwood's *The Handmaid's Tale*, a society that severely mistreats women. The handmaids experience the full weight of oppression at the bottom of society's hierarchy, being used for their bodies and abused. The wives, although married to the commanders, are hushed and silenced, threatened with punishment if they ever attempt to usurp the authority of men. And the commanders, although residing at the top of the hierarchy as men, lead a country that cannot flourish because of the subjugation of its women.

To truly achieve and experience freedom in its fullness, we must all be free. To be connected to each other means that we bear each other's burdens and fight each other's battles. A collectively liberated society is one filled with equity, justice, and peace, where no group is pushed to the margins.

You can choose to pursue collective liberation through the ways you show up for those around you. Every time you raise your voice in opposition to abuse, cast a vote that uplifts the vulnerable, or apply your gifts for the good of others, you extend a hand to another and say, "Let us work together." Together, we get free.

HOME AND
FAMILY

WORK

PLACE OF
WORSHIP

EXAMPLES
OF YOUR
SPHERE OF
INFLUENCE

BUSINESSES
YOU SUPPORT

LOCAL
GOVERNMENT

SCHOOLS,
COLLEGES,
UNIVERSITIES

I VOTED

YO VOTÉ

Sphere of Influence

Each day, you exist in a world that is completely unique to you. Aside from the broader scope of your continent, country, or state, your day-to-day existence is made up of your interactions with your family, friends, roommates, classmates, coworkers, neighbors, congregants, and other groups of people. The communities you're a part of, the places you go, and the people you interact with come together to form your sphere of influence—your area of impact that nobody else has access to.

From the moment you wake up to the time you lay your head down at night, you're given countless opportunities to influence the world around you in meaningful ways. This can look like having inclusive artwork in your home, voting in local elections, standing up for a coworker who's consistently spoken over, or buying a latte at a Black-owned coffee shop. These daily decisions aren't just mundane tasks—they're a beautiful way to cultivate a life that's an extension of your inner values and beliefs.

As much as you're able to influence the community you're surrounded by, you're also formed by the community that surrounds you. Where you work, worship, eat, and learn matters. Our worldviews are shaped by our cultures and experiences, and it's important to always be aware of whether or not our presence and participation in certain places are leading us to become complicit in harm or toxicity. You're allowed to move out of any space that's destructive or not conducive to your flourishing or the flourishing of others.

What a gift it is to be surrounded by this precious community. You have been placed in your sphere of influence for such a time as this. Greet each new day with the awareness of your valuable presence, and live a life that fills the world around you with beauty, truth, and light. When we all awaken to this opportunity, we create room for lasting, meaningful change.

THE KINDS OF PEOPLE

EMPATHIZERS

THROUGH LOW VALLEYS OF DIFFICULTY AND MOUNTAINOUS CHALLENGES, EMPATHIZERS LACE UP THEIR BOOTS AND HIKE ALONGSIDE YOU. THEY AIM TO WALK IN YOUR SHOES AS MUCH AS THEY'RE ABLE AND SEEK TO FEEL YOUR PAIN AS IF IT WERE THEIR OWN.

MOTIVATORS

OUR DREAMS AND GOALS ARE OFTEN EASILY SIDETRACKED. MOTIVATORS COME ALONGSIDE YOU TO CHEER YOU ON, REMIND YOU OF YOUR WORTH, AND HELP YOU KEEP YOUR EYES ON THE PRIZE.

BRAINSTORMERS

STRUGGLING TO GET STARTED? BRAINSTORMERS HELP YOU COME UP WITH IDEAS FOR TACKLING DIFFERENT ASPECTS OF LIFE AND REJUVENATE YOU WHEN YOU'RE FEELING STUCK.

MENTORS

NO MATTER HOW MUCH LIFE YOU'VE EXPERIENCED, YOU NEVER STOP LEARNING. MENTORS TAKE YOU UNDER THEIR WINGS—FILLING YOU WITH ENCOURAGEMENT, ADVICE, AND SUPPORT.

TRUTH-TELLERS

TRUTH-TELLERS WILL ALWAYS KEEP IT REAL. THEY'RE YOUR SECOND SET OF EYES, KEEPING WATCH FOR SIGNS OF DANGER OR OPPORTUNITIES FOR GROWTH, AND THEY ALWAYS HAVE YOUR BEST INTEREST AT HEART.

COMFORTERS

BRING IT IN: COMFORTERS ARE HERE WHEN YOU NEED REASSURING WORDS, A SHOULDER TO CRY ON, OR A REMINDER OF YOUR WORTH.

YOU NEED IN YOUR CIRCLE

PLANNERS

IDEAS ARE GOOD, BUT ACTIVATION GETS THE JOB DONE. PLANNERS HELP YOU GET FROM POINT A TO B AND GIVE YOU ACTION STEPS AND PRACTICAL TIPS FOR THE JOURNEY.

CELEBRATORS

LOOK AT YOU GO! CELEBRATORS NEVER MISS AN OPPORTUNITY TO CONGRATULATE YOU, WHETHER YOU'VE ACCOMPLISHED A GOAL OR MADE IT THROUGH ANOTHER HARD DAY.

LOVERS

WHETHER ROMANTIC, FAMILIAL, OR FRIENDLY, YOU NEED SOMEONE WHO'S GOING TO SHOWER YOU WITH LOVE, CARE, AND AFFECTION. LOVERS MAKE SURE YOU KNOW HOW PRECIOUS YOU ARE.

CONFIDANTS

CONFIDANTS ARE PEOPLE YOU CAN TRUST WITH YOUR THOUGHTS, SECRETS, AND BELIEFS. THEY'RE DEPENDABLE AND KEEP THE DEPTHS OF YOUR HEART UNDER LOCK AND KEY.

ROLE MODELS

ROLE MODELS REMIND US THAT THE GOALS AND DREAMS WE SEEK AREN'T IMPOSSIBLE TO ACHIEVE. THEY'RE SHINING EXAMPLES OF TRAITS AND PRACTICES THAT WOULD BE HELPFUL TO EMULATE.

DREAMERS

SOMETIMES, YOU JUST NEED SOMEONE TO THINK BIG WITH. DREAMERS HELP YOU SEE THE FULLER PICTURE AND CAN ENVISION THOSE IDEAS THAT SEEM TOO OUT OF REACH.

IN COMMUNITY, WE GET

HURT

IN COMMUNITY, WE CAN

HEAL

Sorrow and Safety

Although I was born and raised in a loving family, I was also born and raised in a harmful church system. Week after week, from childhood through college graduation, I'd enter the doors of various churches within the same toxic denomination and be met with spiritual abuse, humiliation, and harmful indoctrination. To this day, healing from that experience is ongoing, requiring many hours of therapy, unlearning, and reconstructing.

After graduating college, one of my first work experiences involved an internship at a small business in a town near mine. From the day I walked in, I experienced a level of care, love, and support that I had never experienced before outside of my family. All I knew was the sorrow of community, but in that season, I learned the safety of community too. With hope restored, I eventually went on to find a new church family—far from the toxic denomination of my youth and full of the love and connection I had always longed for.

What a paradox to be both hurt and healed in community. Being wounded in this context tempts us to self-isolate as we try to avoid the possibility of getting burned again—but we weren't meant to live alone. Regardless of the pain we sometimes experience, people need people. To experience life more fully is to do so hand in hand.

If finding community again after being hurt makes you nervous, remember that beautiful, kind, empathetic people still exist. You deserve to be surrounded by people who listen to you, care about you, and believe in you. Being in community with people who are dedicated to growth and healing unlocks a depth of living that adds more beauty, support, and connection to your life. You're worthy of a safe space.

PEACE ISN'T JUST CALMNESS,
OR THE END OF A FIGHT,

IT'S COMPLETE RESTORATION,
WHERE ALL IS MADE RIGHT.

True Peace

Peace is not calmness. It is not automatically present when all is still. Consider the immediate aftermath of an earthquake or a powerful storm. Buildings have been destroyed, trees fell, and debris and rubble lie everywhere. Yes, all is quiet, but there is not peace—there's devastation. Peace won't be restored in the hearts of those affected until there's repair and restoration, when their belongings are no longer scattered and their homes are inhabitable once again.

A false sense of peace can also show up in our relationships. The silence following a tense argument, apologies left unsaid, tiptoeing around a loved one so as to not awaken the sleeping giant of their rage. In working for justice, false peace can show up as the quiet acceptance of the status quo, where people have chosen calmness instead of the noise of progress.

We must seek peace in its truest form, not the appearance of peace that comes from closing your heart to the world and its troubles. Peace is not found in absence, but in presence.

Peace isn't just calmness or the end of a fight. It's a complete restoration where all is made right. Peace requires repairing relationships, having uncomfortable conversations, and stirring the pot. The pursuit of peace may get messy, noisy, and chaotic, but those who work toward it are closer to peace than those who sit in quiet compliance with the mere appearance of it.

THERE IS SO MUCH
BEAUTY TO BE FOUND

BOTH IN THE DIFFERENCES
THAT SEEK TO DIVIDE US

AND IN THE
HOPEFUL RESILIENCE

THAT WILL
FOREVER CONNECT US

Hopeful Resilience

This is a love letter to women of color: those who battle the two-headed beast of misogyny and racism. We are matriarchs, business owners, makers, and culture shifters. Our bloodlines carry stories—we are women born of women who carved their own paths and navigated generations' worth of challenges.

We see what makes us different. Our cultures are rich and unique, filled with powerful traditions that shape our lives. Each context holds within it generational triumphs and trauma. We've faced our own battles with white supremacy and racism—our ancestral quilts threaded with enslavement, genocide, internment, and asylum. The steps we take to heal are unique to our circumstances.

Yet we also see all that we have in common. We grieve what has been, but we seek to grow into what could be. Whether we're crying out that "Black Lives Matter" or chanting "Stop Asian Hate," we reach across divides and hold space for each other. When the world seeks to move on, step over, look past, or ignore us, we bring each other close, whispering, "I see you, sister." We continuously remember how connected we are—not just in our struggles, but in the ways that we fight through and rise above them.

As long as we have each other, we are not without hope. We are not individual islands—we are bound together. May we be shoulders to lean on, hands to hold, and arms to embrace. May we choose to press on in the face of adversity for the good of us all. There is so much beauty to be found: both in the differences that seek to divide us and in the hopeful resilience that will forever connect us.

A Holy Invitation

I once asked my online community, "What helpful things have other people done for you in difficult seasons?" An overwhelming amount of people recalled times they were welcomed into the spaces of others. They listed examples such as:

"They invited me over."
"They opened their home to me."
"They let me spend time with their families and friends."

It seems that no gift speaks louder than the gift of presence, the tender movement of opening the curtains, exposing a bit of your heart and home in an effort to connect with someone else. It can involve asking someone to get coffee at their favorite spot or taking them to see a movie they've been looking forward to. No matter what you choose, there's something holy and sacred about making room in your heart for others to enter.

As we practice the art of invitation, I challenge you to keep in mind the accompanying posture of openness. A posture of openness says:

"I extend this invitation to you along with the full freedom to decline or change your mind."
"I'm prioritizing your comfort by making it easy for you to say no to this without guilt."
"I'm asking you to come as you are. You don't have to bring the dessert, the drinks, or even paper plates. You just bring you."

A posture of openness allows us to combine the opportunity for connection with the freedom of having no strings attached.

In which ways can you practice the sacred art of invitation in the coming days? Reflect on times you can include someone in conversation or in your presence, then lean into that opportunity. You have been given a holy gift.

UNTIL YOU
FIX IT HERE

AND
ADDRESS
IT HERE

NOTHING
CHANGES
HERE

Family Values

Whether you're a single parent of three, a caregiver for an elderly loved one, or a recent college grad rooming with three of your best friends, the way we view family varies greatly between communities. Regardless of how you define it, it's important to have a shared value system within your family unit.

Shared family values are a guidepost for intentional and impactful living. When you are aware of what you stand for and have committed to actively pursuing those values, you offer up a beautiful gift to the world around you: clear vision and a shared sense of purpose.

There are many ways to come up with this value system. A way to start is by identifying what matters most to each of you and setting aside time to discuss them. Hearing what each person's heart longs for can be a point of connection. You can also bring up your specific passions and desires you have for the future of our society. Creating moments to dream ignites the imagination, and that's what we need to solve some of the issues we face.

Once you've done that, you can put together a list or a manifesto that declares what you want to cultivate in your home and with your family. Put it somewhere where you all will see it daily, using it as a way to start or end your days with clarity and intent. Whether this ends up becoming a family practice or something you do personally, naming your values will help light your way in a world where it's easy to lose sight of what matters most.

LET'S GET LOCAL

VOLUNTEERING	DONATING	GOVERNMENT
JOIN A COMMUNITY CLEAN-UP INITIATIVE	BRING REQUESTED FOODS TO A COMMUNITY FRIDGE	VOTE IN LOCAL AND NATIONAL ELECTIONS
ASSIST OLDER ADULTS THROUGH VISITS TO LONG-TERM CARE FACILITIES	DONATE NEW OR LIGHTLY USED CLOTHING	ASSIST WITH VOTER REGISTRATION EFFORTS
SPEND TIME HELPING AT AN ANIMAL SHELTER	GIVE MONEY TO A LOCAL ORGANIZATION	SERVE AS A POLL WORKER
SUPPORT ORGANIZATIONS THAT WORK WITH UNHOUSED PEOPLE	START YOUR OWN DRIVE COLLECTING ITEMS LIKE FOOD, SOCKS, TOYS, AND COATS	ATTEND CITY MEETINGS
TAKE A SHIFT AT A FOOD BANK OR COMMUNITY FRIDGE	PROVIDE TOILETRIES, TECHNOLOGY, AND RESOURCES TO LOCAL SHELTERS	CONTACT YOUR REPRESENTATIVES TO ENCOURAGE AND SHARE YOUR THOUGHTS

MANY OF US DESIRE TO GET INVOLVED IN OUR LOCAL COMMUNITY, BUT WE DON'T OFTEN KNOW WHERE TO BEGIN. HERE'S A LIST OF 30 WAYS YOU CAN GET PLUGGED IN LOCALLY AND MAKE A DIFFERENCE RIGHT WHERE YOU ARE.

EDUCATION	SMALL BIZ	COMMUNITY SUPPORT
BECOME A MENTOR FOR A CHILD THROUGH A MEMBERSHIP PROGRAM	SHOP AT A SMALL BUSINESS	ATTEND COMMUNITY EVENTS WITH YOUR FAMILY
TUTOR STUDENTS	LEAVE A THOUGHTFUL REVIEW ONLINE	CHECK IN ON YOUR NEIGHBORS
ATTEND SCHOOL BOARD MEETINGS	TAKE A CLASS OR WORKSHOP WHEN THEY'RE OFFERED	STAY INFORMED ON WHAT'S HAPPENING
GET INVOLVED IN A SUMMER CAMP OR READING PROGRAM	SIGN UP FOR A NEWSLETTER	GIVE BLOOD IF YOU'RE ABLE
VOLUNTEER AS A COACH OR SNACK PROVIDER FOR A YOUTH SPORTS TEAM	LEAVE A TIP	ATTEND VIGILS AND PROTESTS

TRUE UNITY follows ACCOUNTABILITY

The Cost of Unity

Unity as a concept is lovely. People from all sorts of backgrounds and affiliations coming together to stand as one sounds like the closing scene of a heartwarming film. For many of us, unity is actually a deep-seated desire and a valuable tool for progress. Yet when we call for unity without counting the cost and taking the necessary steps to actually achieve it, we're glossing over the work it takes to see it come to pass.

Take the game "Mafia," for instance. In this group activity, players sit together in a circle and assume the roles of townspeople. When they close their eyes, members of the group who are secretly part of the mafia open their eyes and plot to eliminate unsuspecting townspeople whose eyes are still closed. When all of the townspeople open their eyes again, they're notified as to which townsperson has been eliminated, and they work together to identify which group members are secretly part of the mafia based on who was eliminated and how other group members are behaving.

In a scenario like this, complete unity among the group is impossible because certain members of the group have a different agenda than others. While the townspeople seek to survive, the secret mafia hidden within their ranks seek to eliminate them. When you apply this concept of unity to our pursuit of justice, we reach a similar end: we cannot achieve unity with all people unless we are united in our desire to do good and prevent harm.

This does not mean that unity is completely elusive. We don't have to completely agree on the methods, but we should certainly agree on the end goal. True unity requires accountability—those who have sought to cause harm taking responsibility and reorienting their lives in pursuit of justice for all.

CONSIS

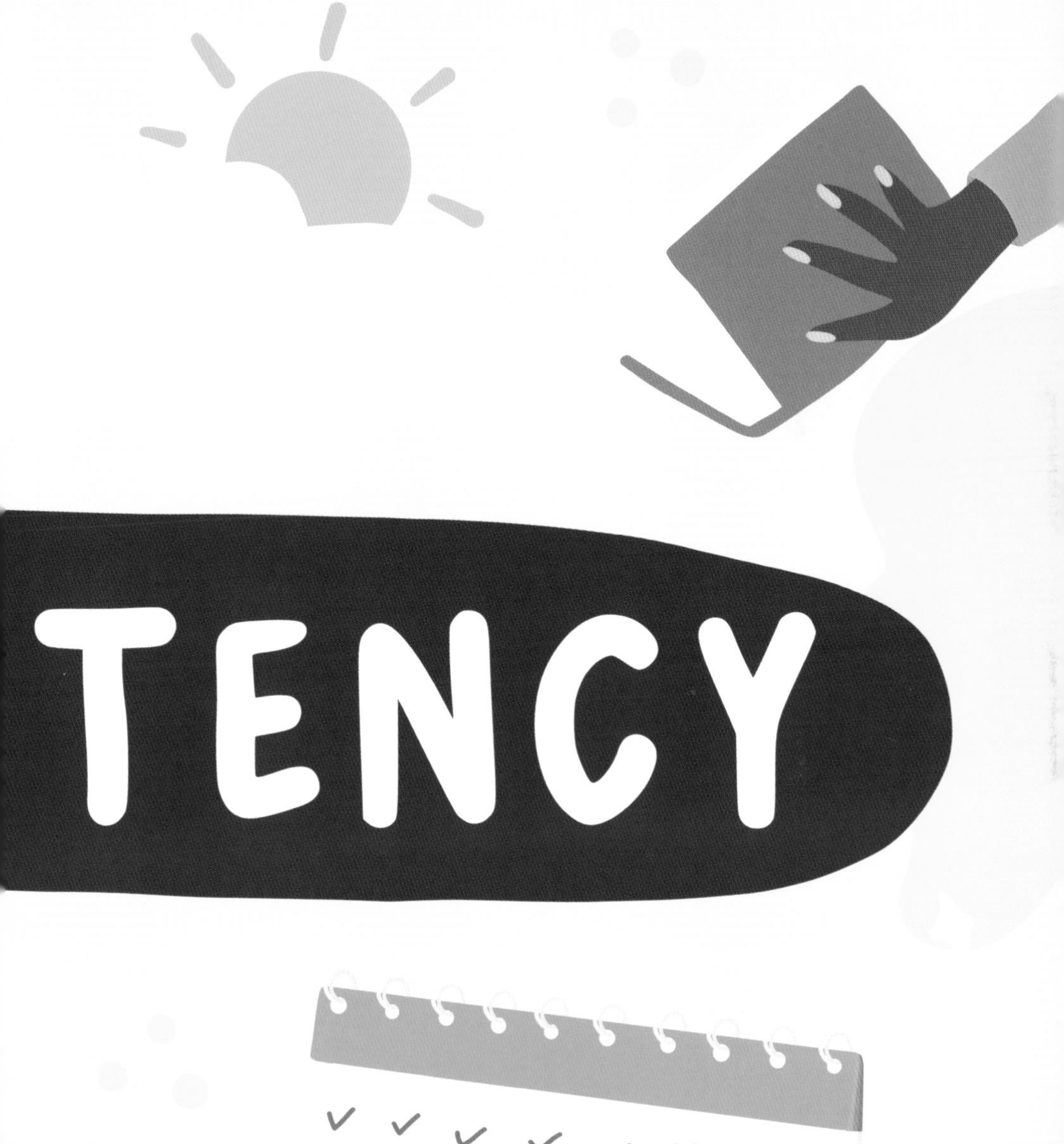
TENCY

WHAT IF YOUR DAYS WEREN'T MARKED BY EXHAUSTING ATTEMPTS AT SPRINTING TO THE FINISH LINE OF PERFECTION, BUT BY A SLOW AND STEADY DEDICATION TO DOING GOOD DAILY, IMPERFECTLY, AND WITH POINTED INTENTION?

Do Good Daily

When we approach our efforts like a sprint each day, it won't be long until the journey of good work feels exhausting. We're going full speed ahead at all times, thinking we have to do "all the things" or it's not enough. We fall into the trap of feeling like the work doesn't matter unless it consists of groundbreaking discoveries, huge donations, or front-page news.

Let's pause right here and take a deep breath. Consider this: what if our days weren't marked by exhausting attempts at sprinting to the finish line of perfection but by doing good daily, imperfectly, and with focused intention?

We could all benefit from focusing on simple ways to cultivate a daily habit of good work. We can start by separating this into two categories: thinking and learning.

The mind informs everything we do. If I do not think rightly about myself, treat myself with compassion, or make a habit of thinking good thoughts, I'll make a mess within my mind. Because of this, a helpful strategy could involve starting every day with setting intentions and readying ourselves for targeted, direct action. Try thinking about an impactful quote, Scripture, or passage and write it down for reflection. What is one truth I can continuously remember? What lovely thought can I meditate on? The way we begin our mornings often sets the trajectory for our days.

Cultivating a daily habit of good work also requires learning. As much as you're able, look for opportunities to create rhythms of learning by reading portions of a book, researching a recent news headline, or watching snippets of a documentary.

Thinking and learning are important practices that help us pursue a life of good work through meaningful daily habits. In time, we'll find ourselves with a greater sense of awareness and a posture of continuous learning that motivates us to seek progress in all things.

EYES ON THE PRIZE

REWARDS FOR LIVING A LIFE OF ALIGNMENT

INTEGRITY

CLARITY

PEACE

FULFILLMENT

CREDIBILITY

A Life of Alignment

I will never forget what it felt like to fire a client for the first time. It was both horrific and glorious—and it was absolutely necessary.

For context, I ran a successful social media agency for years before I focused exclusively on illustration. The mission was simple: helping positive, mission-based brands use social media for maximum impact. I connected with all sorts of organizations and individuals who were so busy doing good work that they didn't have enough time to focus on crafting an aesthetically pleasing social media presence—which is where I came in to help.

One client relationship, in particular, started out like a dream. They were a nonprofit with a mission to encourage people to become activists and spread positive messaging about using your voice to make a difference. Yet behind closed doors, the founder of the organization was abrasive, demeaning, and rude to me throughout the course of our partnership. In order to stay aligned with my mission of helping organizations and individuals who were dedicated to doing good—both online and in real life—I had to let this client go. My pockets got a little bit lighter, but so did my spirit.

Being consistent with your desire to live a life of purpose requires dedication to staying aligned with the values you hold dear. A healthy moral compass doesn't lie, and if we start to veer off course, it will guide us back and remind us of our North Star. It's our responsibility to pay attention and find our way back home.

No dollar amount, valuable connection, or momentary benefit is worth the cost of misalignment. When you keep your eyes on the prize of progress, your rewards are much more meaningful: peace, integrity, and credibility that will convince others to join you in the real, lifelong work.

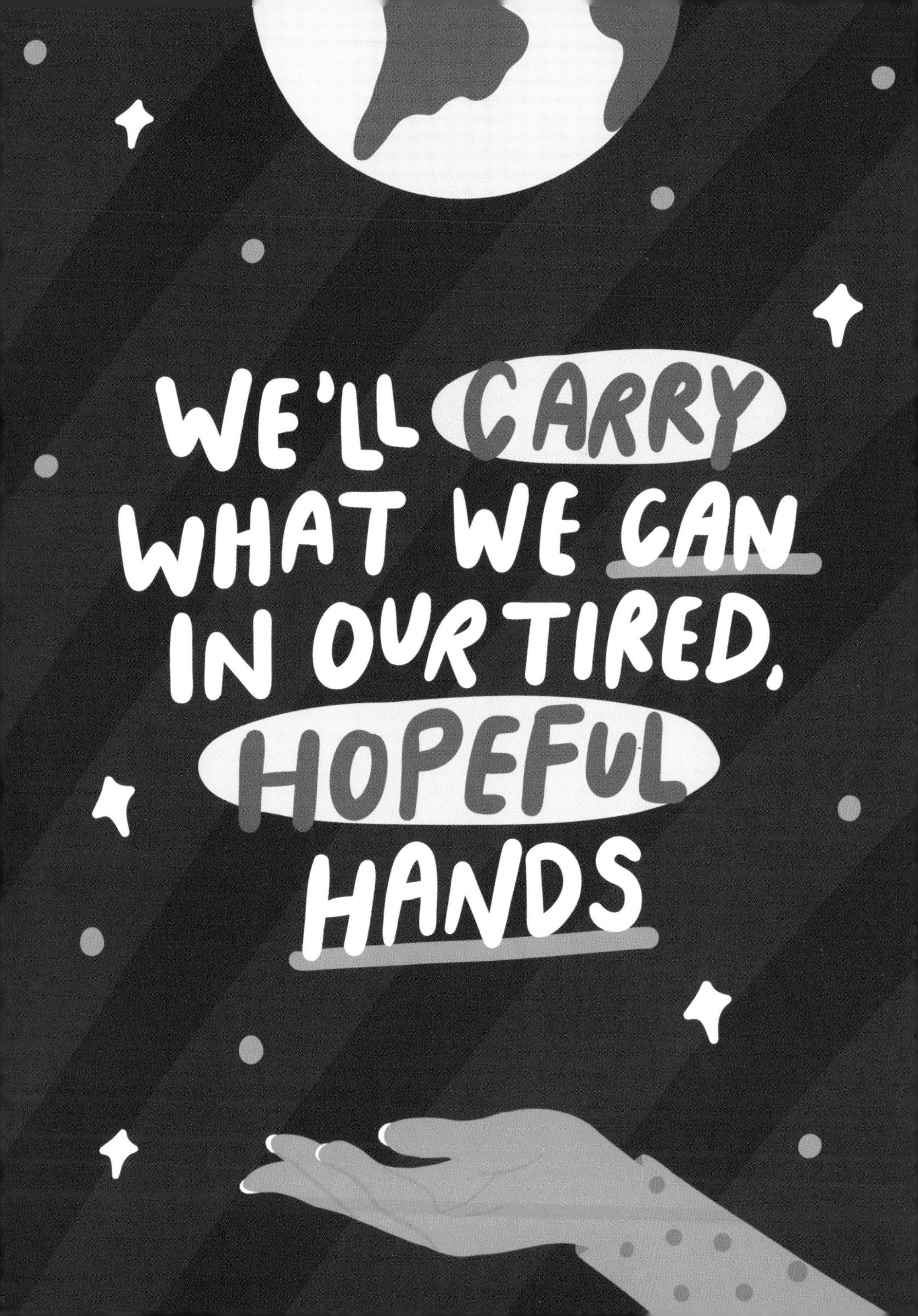
WE'LL CARRY
WHAT WE CAN
IN OUR TIRED,
HOPEFUL
HANDS

Carry What You Can

As the hardships of any given day fall like leaves from trees rooted in oppression, inequity, and hardship, some leaves will inevitably slip through your grasp. You cannot give attention to every leaf. They cannot all be held, but there are many that can be. When any overwhelming feeling sinks in and it seems like we can affect little or no positive change, remember what's within your reach: your loved ones, your neighbors, and the small ways you can make a difference.

Each day, you have an opportunity to positively influence your loved ones through acts of kindness, providing comfort during tough times, and embodying your core values. As you pursue a life of good work, lean into opportunities to fill your loved ones' days with support and joy.

In a slightly broader sense, think about people you encounter on a daily, weekly, or monthly basis. Being intentional about doing good where you're planted is an opportunity to water the seeds of change around you and watch them grow. Even when you don't feel like your reach is wide enough, you're needed right where you are.

We all have causes and issues that we naturally connect to. We can't fix everything, but we can take small steps to spark change right where we are. Local involvement, digital awareness, donations, and so many other practical actions have incredible, positive effects. Nobody can impact an issue you care about like you can.

It's okay that you can't hold it all; you weren't meant to. Whatever falls into your hands, be kind to yourself first, then find ways to carry what you can.

5 THINGS TO REMIND YOURSELF OF AFTER MAKING A MISTAKE

I DID THE BEST I COULD WITH THE INFORMATION I HAD AT THE TIME

MISTAKES ARE NATURAL BUMPS ON THE JOURNEY OF BEING HUMAN

PERFECTION IS UNATTAINABLE & A CRUEL STANDARD TO HOLD MYSELF TO

MY LEARNINGS WILL BECOME A BLUEPRINT FOR FUTURE DECISIONS

THIS MOMENT DOES NOT DEFINE ME. I AM MORE THAN MY MISSTEPS.

On Mistakes

Mistakes can feel all-consuming. We replay that thing we said or that decision we made over and over until we're drowning in guilt and shame, wondering if we're even cut out for living a life of good work. One thing you can take comfort in is that mistakes are factored into the journey. Your twists and turns are factored in and expected. It's what you do after the mistake is made that determines your trajectory. Here are a few things to remember when you're feeling discouraged:

"I did the best I could with the information I had at the time."
You are not an evil person who spends your days dreaming up ways to cause chaos or treat people horribly. The decisions you made are often a result of your best intentions and a sum of what you knew at that moment. If you receive new information afterward, then great! You're now able to course-correct and do things differently. Give yourself grace for what you didn't know.

"My learnings will become a blueprint for future decisions."
Your brain takes mental notes after mistakes. Don't throw away what you have learned in shame; instead, use learnings as a map for your journey. You now know which turns to avoid and which paths are not safe. You've given your internal compass updated information. Find encouragement in the fact that your lessons inform your next steps and that you're consistently learning.

"This moment does not define me. I am more than my missteps."
Whatever the mistake, it is not the sum of you. You are a dreamer, an empath, an encourager, a fighter, a friend, and a human being. There is so much more to you than any mishap that may keep you up at night. Missteps are natural bumps on the journey of being human, and you make this world a more beautiful place each time you decide to get back up and try again.

I WON'T BECOME ADDICTED TO SEEKING EXTERNAL VALIDATION

I CHOOSE SHARING OVER COMPARING

I CAN'T FIND FULFILLMENT HERE

I DON'T NEED A FOLLOWING TO OFFER GOOD TO THE WORLD

I WILL RESIST ENDLESS DOOMSCROLLING

THIS IS A TOOL, NOT A MEASURING STICK

"LIKES" DO NOT DEFINE ME

THINGS TO REMEMBER ABOUT SOCIAL MEDIA:

OHHAPPYDANI Posts

ohhappydani

View Insights

Finding Fulfillment

What keeps a painter coming back to their palette, a baker to her oven, a writer to his pen? The love of it. Being in love with what you do makes the doing much more alluring. It calls to you when you're away and fills your heart with joy when you're near. It's here where we find a sense of fulfillment—satisfaction and contentment—in our lives and offerings. This is often what keeps us going.

There's an enticing distraction in our society that tends to pull us away from what we love in an effort to be more seen, more known, and more successful. This is social media—platforms created for us to share what we love. But often, they end up acting as voids and vortexes, consistently sucking us into endless scrolling, comparing, and searching. We yearn to be validated and celebrated, often at the cost of our own sense of worth and fulfillment.

There is beauty in sharing what we love with others. That's a big part of creating—filling the world with beauty and light. Yet when our mediums become more like measuring sticks, we start to lose our spark and our desire to do what brings us joy.

Do you lie awake at night, dreaming with open eyes about a world beyond likes and algorithms and the pressure to keep up? Do you have a hopeful imagination about a world you cannot yet touch with your hands but can see with your heart? These feeds, pages, and online spaces will not satisfy you. Use them, but do not let them use you.

Fulfillment won't be found in comment sections or notifications or other people's expectations, but in the steady seeking of what we were created for, and the pursuit of what comes alive in our hearts as we dream.

INNER ROADBLOCKS

ON THE JOURNEY OF GOOD WORK

OVERWHELM

COMPARISON

FEAR OF FAILURE

SELF DOUBT

FEAR OF JUDGMENT

Inner Roadblocks

With every good idea or intention meant to help us move forward, there's an inner obstacle that tries to hold us back. Most of the time, we're our own greatest obstacles—lying to ourselves, talking ourselves out of an idea, and allowing fear to control our actions. Let's explore some of the most common inner roadblocks and work toward overcoming them.

Self-Doubt

You may not feel fully equipped, knowledgeable, or 100 percent confident, but rest in this: liberation happens in community, where your efforts are joined with the power of the collective. In the places where you fall short, be reminded that there are others working right alongside you, helping to fill in the gaps and contribute in their own unique ways. You're not alone.

Guilt and Shame

Feeling guilty before you undertake good work is more common than you might think. Many of us wish we could do more, or we beat ourselves up for what we haven't done in the past. Know that what you bring to the table today is worthy and enough; you're not defined by your past actions or lack thereof. Be confident in your contribution and show up with your whole heart—what you have to offer is exactly what we've been waiting for.

Fear of Judgment

If you step out in bravery to take action, chances are others will witness your endeavors and be inspired or energized by your initiative. Taking action is always a risk, and putting a piece of your heart on display for those around you takes courage and vulnerability. The good news is that more people are in your corner than you realize. Be encouraged that your bravery is positively influencing someone else whether you're aware of it or not.

Working through our inner roadblocks prevents the lies we tell ourselves from having the final say. When we free ourselves, we're able to free others too.

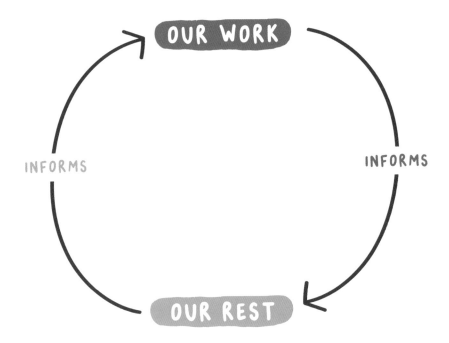

We Work from Rest

Rest is not a reward. You do not earn it after the completion of a task or at a certain time each night. Rest is not a luxury, something we'd only acquire with enough resources or time. Rest is a necessity, a gift. It refreshes our creativity and recharges our abilities. With rest, we are able to reap the most beauty and sustenance from our days.

Howard Thurman, mentor to Dr. Martin Luther King Jr., regarded work and rest as two sides of the same coin. Viewing rest and work as conjoined brings a sense of stability to our days and aids us in continuously walking out our purpose. We bring what we gain from rest into our work: a sense of patience, a steady hand, a spirit less flustered, and a heart less anxious. We aren't forced to hurriedly hustle or move at the pace of culture because we are not fueled by a need to produce.

We bring what we gain from work into our rest: dreaming up new ways to flood this earth with beauty, adding our day's observations to our lists of prayers and meditation. This is not consistently thinking of work and what's next on our to-do lists, but a reminder that rest itself is part of good work.

You can believe that you were created to do good and also know that living a life poured out is unsustainable if you're not pouring into yourself too. A rested you is a more balanced you. It increases your capacity for gentleness and patience, it lengthens your fuse, it brings you back to your center. Don't let your desire to do as much good as possible rob you of this lovely gift. Let rest expand your ability to love and live fully.

From Burning to Burnout

The journey of good work often begins with the best intentions. A spark quickly turns into a fire, lighting us up to live a life of action, intentionality, and love. However, no matter how bright the flame, we risk burning out due to the intensity and rigor of the race we run.

Burnout is complete exhaustion that puts an extended pause on our output. It's an internal crash that puts all of our systems on red alert, signaling to us that something is wrong within. Burnout can show up for several reasons, but here are two to take notice of as you live out your purpose each day: feeling overwhelmed and suffering from trauma.

There will always be work to do, and the work will continue on—with or without you. This truth needs to sink in as you consider your contribution to the world around you. This doesn't mean that your offering doesn't have value; actually, it's a reminder that you are only one person and you cannot save the world. Cover yourself with compassion. Do what you can relative to your capacity, remembering that it's okay to slow down or pause to rest.

It's also important to acknowledge the weight of the work on your mind, body, and soul. If you're attempting to improve the world on any level, you'll undoubtedly bear witness to its brokenness. You are worthy of a whole and healed life, and you can make space for that on your journey.

There will be those who try to convince you that there's no time to stop for rest on the changemaker's path. Be reminded that we're running a marathon, not a sprint, and you owe it to yourself to run this race well.

STEP BY STEP

DAY BY DAY

Keep the Faith

America's Civil Rights Movement throughout the 1950s and '60s is a shining example of longsuffering. The Montgomery Bus Boycott lasted for 382 days, while Freedom Rides occurred for months throughout 1961. From marches to sit-ins, protests against racism were known to be long, grueling, and sometimes even deadly.

Of the many lessons that can be pulled from this era, one of the most notable is the stamina portrayed by the many participants of the movement. They were often subjected to insults, harassment, and physical attacks, yet they remained steadfast in their pursuit of integration and rights for the Black community.

We ourselves are no strangers to suffering while pursuing the greater good. From strained relationships to oppression under unjust systems, we're wanting to press on in the face of great difficulty, but the reality is it's a great challenge.

How did our ancestors build up this stamina? It seems that it came from many different places. Many of them found strength in the power of community, locking arms in the face of overwhelming circumstances and meeting together as often as they could. They also trained extensively, building up their tolerance for abuse and harassment before actually facing it. One thing a great majority of them possessed was faith in the idea that change was possible, along with hope in a future that was different from their present.

When you find it difficult to persevere in the face of difficulty, remember that you're in good company. Many came before us and showed us the power of keeping the faith and powering through adversity. There is strength in the belief that a better future can be built, and as long as we work toward it, we are moving the needle forward to see that dream become a reality.

YOUR JOY IS YOUR RIGHT

The Right to Joy

In the Declaration of Independence, the Founding Fathers penned, "We hold these truths to be self-evident, that all men are created equal, that they are endowed by their Creator with certain unalienable Rights, that among these are Life, Liberty and the pursuit of Happiness."

Throughout history, changemakers have worked to make this statement ring true for all people. We fight for equity to eventually arrive at equality and to ensure that historically excluded communities have a fair shot at life. Yet one area that often goes overlooked is the pursuit of happiness. In doing what we can to free ourselves from the joy-snatching grip of oppression, we find happiness often slips from our grasp too.

One thing Black activists fought for during civil rights protests of the '60s was the right to enjoy places of amusement. It wasn't enough to integrate restaurants and water fountains; they also wanted to enjoy swimming pools, amusement parks, and theaters. A sit-in on a carousel was as important as a sit-in at a lunch counter because denying the right to recreation was just as dehumanizing, if not more so.

As a Black woman, choosing joy and delight is a powerful act of resistance. It's a reclamation of my self-evident, unalienable right. In a world that seeks to take and take, choosing pleasure is a reminder to myself that I am more than what I produce. My access to joy is not transactional.

Clinging to delight while fighting for change is a radical act. It's refusing to reduce your own quality of life while working to make life better for everyone. Joy is a slice of the fruit of the Spirit, a flicker of hope that carries us through moments of despair, and a reminder of what is good in a world that aims to deter us with its evil. In choosing happiness, we choose resistance, hope, and fortitude, and we remind others that we are free to exist in our fullness.

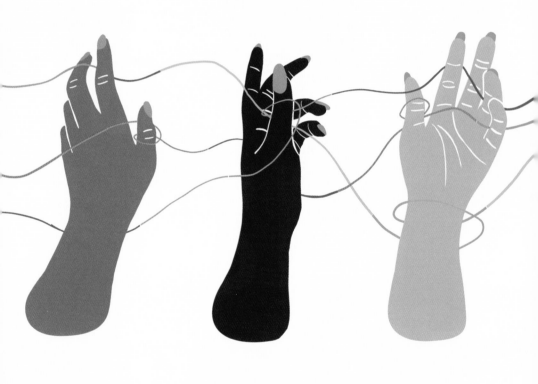

The Strings That Tie Us

What a gift it is to be connected to each other. Our experiences tie together like a pile of tangled strings—distinct but difficult to separate. Regardless of the path we're walking, someone in this world is unknowingly walking in tandem, feeling similar grief, joy, disappointment, excitement, or heartbreak.

This reality presents us with both a comfort and a call. We're comforted in the truth that we are not alone in the trials we face, and that it's possible to find a sense of belonging and relief when we identify someone who can walk through the valleys of life with us. On the other hand, we're called to be open to being that person who can give that gift of belonging and relief to another.

Life presents countless opportunities to trace the strings that tie us. Every conversation, online post, or text message leaves a trail, and there will come a point when we feel that small tug to offer connection or support. Perhaps a friend is experiencing the valley of a relationship's end and you've successfully conquered your own heartbreak, or a parent just got laid off from their job and you've waded through the waters of uncertainty, making it to the other side. These moments of discovery are when you can spot the strings.

At the same time, when you feel the pull of someone else's offer to support and connect with you, allow yourself to receive it. You were not made to fight the battles of this life alone. Find comfort in the certainty of the strings—the guarantee that there is someone in this life who has wandered down a similar road. Whether it's through a book, phone call, message board, or support group, allow the strings of relatability between you and others to form a quilt of comfort and safety as you continue wandering down the paths of life.

"IT'S TOUGH WALKING IN THESE SHOES."

SYMPATHY SAYS:
"I'M SO SORRY ABOUT THAT. I SEE YOU & I CARE."

EMPATHY SAYS:
"I FEEL THIS WITH YOU & CAN UNDERSTAND IT."

(WALKING IN THEIR SHOES AS MUCH AS YOU'RE ABLE)

COMPASSION SAYS:
"I'M MOVED TO ACT ON YOUR BEHALF & HELP."

Sympathy, Empathy, Compassion

All of us are participants in the human experience, with varying degrees of hardship and trials—many of which are exacerbated by injustice and inequity. Sympathy is the recognition of pain, injustice, and inequity in the life of a fellow human being. Sympathy pulls at our heartstrings, but there are times when empathy beckons to us and says, "There is more required of you here."

Empathy, the bearing of another's burdens through shared feeling, takes sympathy a step further. To empathize is to do more than recognize someone's pain, it's to relate to a struggle on a personal level. Empathy connects you to the emotions of others and personalizes your response. Feeling someone's mourning as your own naturally makes you more invested in their liberation—that's why empathy increases our power to do good work in our spheres of influence and areas of passion.

Picture the human body: if empathy is the heart, compassion is the hands. Compassion combines the emotional connection of empathy with a willingness to take action and help. It's why we hold fundraisers, stock community fridges, and speak out on behalf of those experiencing oppression. Compassion sparks change.

Every day we're presented with someone who says, "It's tough walking in these shoes." Sympathy says, "I'm so sorry about that. I see you and I care." Empathy responds, "I feel this with you and can understand it." Compassion adds, "I'm moved to act on your behalf and help."

All three of these expressions of care are important and necessary. As imperfect humans, we won't always have the capacity to act in support of every worthy cause. It's my hope, however, that we'll strive to walk in another's shoes whenever we're able. May our sympathy, our empathy, and our compassion lead us toward action on behalf of those who need us most.

IT SHOULDN'T HAVE TO HAPPEN TO YOU FOR IT TO MATTER TO YOU

It Should Matter

The kind of empathy discussed most often is the up-close-and-personal type. It's putting yourself in the shoes of another, often identifying with them based on factors like proximity or your own lived experiences. Yet there are times when life asks us to empathize with those whose lives look nothing like our own. We hear of the trials faced by those who are separate from us, whether demographically or geographically, and we come face-to-face with our own capacities to empathize.

It shouldn't have to happen to you for it to matter to you. Our empathy should extend beyond issues that directly affect us. This does not mean absorbing all of the world's difficulties like a sponge, becoming heavy with the load of what we soak in. Instead, it's a reminder for our hearts to remain soft and open. When we harden ourselves to the struggles of others, we become less inclined to work for progress on their behalf when the opportunity presents itself.

In some ways, the ability to empathize with others is a privilege in and of itself. How fortunate we are to not have to experience the full magnitude of life's many horrors. We ourselves do not move through life unscathed, but we do have the ability to recognize when others are being scorched by flames of grief, pain, or terror. And, as much as we're able, we have a responsibility to respond.

This kind of empathy practices curiosity. It makes a habit of investigating, seeking, and listening. When you meet the limits of your own understanding, empathy takes the lead, filling in the gaps with what we already know to be true based on our shared humanity: we each deserve to be heard, fought for, and protected.

The Weight of Compassion

It can seem, at times, that we're caught in an endless loop of trauma. News cycles, social media doomscrolls, and our own personal hardships circle around in our minds until we find ourselves feeling overwhelmed and hopeless. Our hearts feel stretched in multiple directions, our empathy begins to wear thin, and we scold ourselves for feeling the weight of compassion.

There's a phrase for this phenomenon—compassion fatigue—and it's normally used in reference to caregivers, doctors, nurses, therapists, and similar professions that are up close and personal with life's most traumatic experiences. Yet there's a version of this experience that can creep into the life of the everyday person who practices empathy and is rocked by society's consistent onslaught of despair.

We must find a way to allow compassion to move through us without crushing us. One way to move toward this would be to divide the weight of it among those who walk with us through life. A sign of true community is the ability to collectively shoulder life's heavy loads so that no single person is completely crushed.

Another strategy for carrying compassion involves a dedication to personal well-being. When we prioritize our mental and physical health, spiritual practices, joyful hobbies, and times of rest, we pour into ourselves and fill our own cups. Caring for our own bodies and minds keeps us steady and strong—and when it's time to pour into others, we won't have to do it at the expense of our own well-being.

When lifting a heavy box, there are automatic considerations: How heavy is it? Do I have the strength? Will I need help? How long am I carrying this? How far am I able to go? It would do us well to consider similar questions as we do compassion's heavy lifting.

ENCOURAGEMENT STARTER PACK

IDEAS FOR SHOWING SUPPORT DURING HARD TIMES

SOLIDIFY YOUR PRESENCE
AND HOLD SPACE FOR
THEIR NEEDS

ACKNOWLEDGE THE
DIFFICULTY OF THE SITUATION
AND VALIDATE THEIR EMOTIONS

THIS IS
SO HARD

AND I'M
SO SORRY.

GOT YA SOME
GROCERIES!

ANTICIPATE THEIR NEEDS AND
PLAN AN INTENTIONAL ACT OF
KINDNESS

LEAN INTO YOUR PROXIMITY BY
PROVIDING PERSONALIZED
ENCOURAGEMENT THAT FITS
THEIR SPECIFIC NEEDS

When Words Fail

Many of us desire to truly be sources of support and comfort for our loved ones when they find themselves in tough seasons. We grapple with the fear of saying the wrong thing or being unhelpful, and sometimes this holds us back from saying or doing anything altogether. When considering how to be there for someone else, there are a few things we can focus on to start with: acknowledgment, validation, and anticipation.

In the middle of a hard situation, it's easy for someone to belittle their hardship as not being "that bad" or feel guilty for drawing attention. When we acknowledge our loved one's difficulty, we're letting them know that we see them and the storm that they're in. It's saying, "Yes, this is hard, and I'm so sorry." A simple acknowledgment can go a long way for someone who may be feeling like their struggles don't matter.

Similarly, validation involves confirming that their emotions are justifiable. It's letting them know that they have a right to feel how they feel. Many of us are tempted to shove our emotions down, ignoring the very real impact of hardship in our lives. To feel justified in your emotions gives you a sense of freedom in expressing them.

Anticipation involves thinking ahead to ways you can physically show your support for your loved one in need. It involves leaning on your relationship with this person, recalling things like their favorite foods or chores they may find difficult, and discovering ways to lighten their load. Anticipating needs demonstrates a sense of intentionality and care that speaks volumes about the love you have for someone else.

At the end of the day, there's no "right" way to encourage someone else, and words often fail us. Even so, there are ways to show those we love that we see them and are moved to compassionate acts on their behalf. It may sometimes seem like nothing we say will actually help, but learning how to love well during hardship is part of the long journey toward cultivating a life of empathy.

the art of
HOLDING SPACE

CREATING A CIRCLE OF SAFETY
TO FACILITATE SUPPORT

EXCHANGING "DEVIL'S ADVOCACY"
AND "WHATABOUTISM" FOR EMPATHY
AND COMPASSION

LEANING INTO COMMUNITY AND
CENTERING THOSE IN NEED

PRIORITIZING PHYSICAL, MENTAL, AND
EMOTIONAL PRESENCE OVER JUDGMENT

Holding Space

As I've walked through difficult seasons with friends and family, I've learned four simple ways to practice holding space—being fully present for someone without judgment:

Create a circle of safety to facilitate support.
In times of hardship, the circle of safety can ensure that the person you're supporting feels protected and welcomed, whether it's meant to provide them with joy or simply exists to listen to their needs. The circle of safety promotes vulnerability and openness instead of isolation and loneliness, making difficult journeys a little easier to walk.

Exchange "what about-ism" and devil's advocacy for empathy and compassion.
When a jarring headline hits the news, an onslaught of opinions always follows. But how do we handle headlines that describe the pain and grief of an entire community that we don't identify with? The art of holding space requires pushing back against our natural inclination to ask, "What about this?" or say, "Let me play devil's advocate for a second." It asks us to resist making our voices the loudest in the room.

Lean into community and center those in need.
To center someone is to focus on their experience instead of your own. It means saying "no" to giving unsolicited advice, inserting personal anecdotes, or listening just to respond—deciding that the well-being of the suffering person takes precedence over others' need to be "right."

Prioritize physical, mental, and emotional presence over judgment.
When someone makes a decision we don't agree with, it's easy to come in hot with our judgments and opinions. Holding space for someone else involves coming in neutral, creating a judgment-free zone where people feel safe. Instead of pointing with one finger, try embracing with two hands, opening your ears and your heart to make space for healing and growth to take place.

On Solidarity and Allyship

It's a beautiful notion to want to stand in solidarity with another group or community. We see it in history—countries partnering together to fight against the tyranny of other nations, or people of different ethnicities marching for Black lives. Solidarity involves locking arms across dividing lines to actively advocate for the well-being of people on the margins. While seeking to do this well, there are a few things to keep in mind that can strengthen solidarity efforts and dignify affected communities.

The title of an ally isn't self-appointed. Allyship isn't validated by the ally themself, but by the group of people who they seek to partner with. In working toward progress, the community on the margins are the experts of their own needs and collective vision for true, meaningful change. The ally does not swoop in to save, nor do they view their own ideas and methods as superior—they step in to help move the collective vision forward.

Allyship is a journey, not a destination. The title of an ally is not the end goal. The end goal is justice and the achievement of the desired change, which often takes time, effort, and patience. To arrive at the "end" of allyship is to say that the work is fully complete, but shifting to a mindset of a journey is a reminder that it's a process with ups and downs, mistakes and gains—full of imperfection but never-ending.

Solidarity involves initiative. The burden lies on the ally to self-educate, listen, and course correct. This is not leading the charge but following the blueprint that's already been created and lending their own privilege to the advancement of the affected community's goals.

We are the experts of our own life experiences. When we reach across to support other communities, we remember this truth, knowing that our collective action seeks to bring meaningful change for those who need it most.

THE ACTIVE LISTENER

IN TIMES OF DIFFICULTY, THE PRESENCE OF A CARING AND EMPATHETIC LISTENER CAN BE A BEAUTIFUL GIFT. AS YOU SEEK TO LOVE WELL WITH YOUR PRESENCE, HERE ARE A FEW TIPS THAT ARE BOTH PRACTICAL AND INTENTIONAL FOR THOSE PRECIOUS MOMENTS:

EYE CONTACT IS POWERFUL. IT COMMUNICATES TO YOUR LOVED ONE THAT THEY HAVE YOUR FULL ATTENTION AND ARE SEEN IN THE MOMENT.

LISTEN TO UNDERSTAND, NOT RESPOND. FOCUSING ON WHAT YOU'RE GOING TO SAY NEXT CAN DISTRACT FROM THE OPPORTUNITY TO FULLY GRASP WHAT'S BEING SHARED WITH YOU.

GAIN CONSENT BEFORE PROVIDING ADVICE. OFTEN, SOMEONE IS SIMPLY LOOKING TO SHARE HOW THEY'RE FEELING AND ARE NOT NECESSARILY SEEKING A FIX.

DON'T UNDERESTIMATE THE POWER OF VERBAL CUES. THIS KIND OF VALIDATION CAN GO A LONG WAY AND REMINDS YOUR LOVED ONE THAT THEIR WORDS AREN'T GOING IN ONE EAR AND OUT THE OTHER.

ASK CLARIFYING QUESTIONS. PROMPTS LIKE "ARE YOU LOOKING TO VENT RIGHT NOW?" HELPS YOU GAUGE THE POSTURE OF YOUR LOVED ONE AND THOUGHTFULLY ENGAGE.

ACTIVE LISTENING IS MORE THAN HEARING WORDS, IT ALSO INVOLVES READING NONVERBAL CUES AND BODY LANGUAGE. YOU'LL BE MORE EQUIPPED TO ANTICIPATE AND RESPOND TO THEIR NEEDS—WHETHER IT'S GRABBING SOME TISSUE BEFORE THEY START TO CRY OR NOTICING IF THE CONVERSATION NEEDS TO GO IN A DIFFERENT DIRECTION.

DO YOUR BEST TO RESERVE JUDGMENT. SHARING OFTEN REQUIRES VULNERABILITY AND CAN FEEL LIKE YOU'RE EXPOSING YOURSELF TO ALL KINDS OF OPINIONS. SHARP CRITIQUE OR HARSH FEEDBACK CAN HAVE A DEVASTATING EFFECT ON YOUR LOVED ONE IN THESE MOMENTS OF TRANSPARENCY.

SHOW THAT YOU UNDERSTAND, EVEN IF YOU DON'T FULLY SHARE THE SAME EXPERIENCES OR PERSPECTIVES. USE REPETITION, REFLECTION, AND SUMMARIZATION. THIS CAN VALIDATE YOUR LOVED ONE'S FEELINGS AND HELP THEM FEEL SEEN.

WE FIND CONNECTION IN THE STORIES WE SHARE

Storytelling and Empathy

When my artwork first started circulating on social media, I was intrigued. As a graphic designer with a marketing background and a desire to see us all grow in empathy, I was curious about why people seemed to be drawn to my artwork in droves. This began my journey into studying the impact of artivism and visual communication.

Early in my research, I learned that illustration is distinctly tied to feelings of nostalgia and familiarity. When we view illustrated artwork, we're transported back in time to the stories told in our favorite cartoon shows and children's books. What we learned back then is just as relevant today: storytelling is a powerful tool for learning. We remember the lessons taught to us by fairy-tale heroes and the moral at the end of every story. Those connections stay with us and are reignited by certain types of visual art.

This helps to explain why artivism—art as activism—is so effective today. Art seeks to invoke emotion, while activism encourages action. When combined, we have a powerful tool that encourages action by invoking emotion. The key to all of it is storytelling: inviting the audience into the art and helping them envision the role that they play in the larger story of justice and good work. It's one thing to give someone a to-do list, and it's another thing entirely to invite them into a story and let them discover their own action steps.

When it comes to empathy, storytelling helps us put on the shoes of another and become immersed in their world. Whether it's through verbal sharing, film, or illustrated infographics, storytelling creates opportunities to decenter ourselves and focus on the lived experiences of others. As you seek to grow in empathy, look for ways to sit with someone else's story and allow your emotional response to blossom into tangible action.

THE MORE THE HEART LEARNS,

THE MORE THE HEART GROWS.

Empathy in Motion

How can we practically grow in empathy? As much as we'd like to be pros at this, it's often easier said than done. We improve in this area when we treat empathy as a muscle—building it up with dedicated practice and putting it to use so it remains strong.

A simple way to begin practicing empathy is to pay more attention to the people we interact with each day. We can better feel what another person is feeling when we have a clear understanding of how they feel in the first place. Paying closer attention to others during conversations helps us get better at reading them. Similarly, opening ourselves up to conversations with new people can improve our empathy by unlocking our minds to perspectives and opinions we may not have held ourselves. Being exposed to different ways of thinking equips us to show up for others in new ways.

Another way to grow in empathy is to pay more attention to what is happening in the world around you. It's one thing to hear about a disaster or tough situation, but it's another to take in personal accounts of what's happening and how others are responding. Watching video interviews, reading up on the work of different nonprofits and causes, and talking to people who may be affected are a few ways to expand your empathy and grow in your understanding of the realities of life for those around you.

Our ability to grow in empathy is directly related to our willingness to work at it. Muscle-building is rarely comfortable, and we may find ourselves facing discomfort when the work of practicing empathy involves weeding out our own biases or preconceived notions. In the end, putting empathy in motion in our own lives will have a ripple effect that inevitably improves the lives of others too.

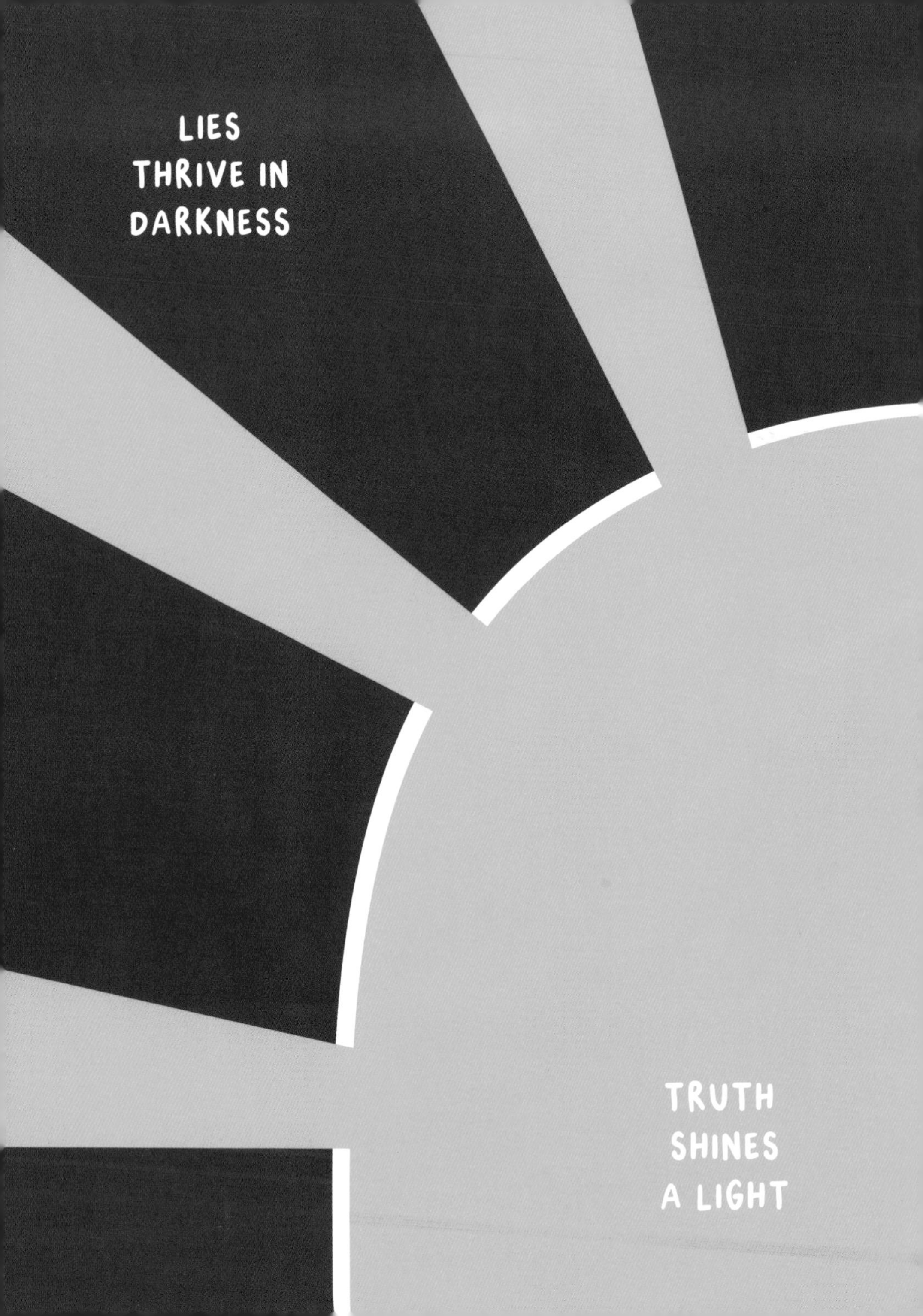
LIES
THRIVE IN
DARKNESS
TRUTH
SHINES
A LIGHT

Two Truths and No Lies

You cannot do good work without telling the truth.

I often describe the act of doing good work as flooding darkness with light. Oppression often persists because somewhere someone is lying—and unjust systems, along with their perpetuators, thrive in the darkness of false narratives.

One of the ways we drown out the darkness of dishonesty is by using our own voices, and lives, to shine a light of truth. I would describe this personal responsibility of honesty as twofold: telling the truth of our own stories and being wholeheartedly dedicated to facts.

To tell the truth of your own story is to shine the light of your own lived experience. Nothing is truer to you than your own journey. Maybe you've experienced the difficulty of being the only Black employee in your predominantly white place of business, or you've experienced discrimination when trying to receive adequate healthcare. Regardless of what your story is, within it lies a truth that can't be denied: you have lived through this. Using your voice to share the truth of your own journey is a powerful tool against oppression.

Additionally, we bear the duty of protecting facts. The truth is the truth, regardless of how others react to it. Being dedicated to the truth is what enables us to be credible, hold others accountable, and push back against deception. In a world where people seek to distort, hide, and cloud reality, it's up to us to be beacons of honesty—pointing others to a better way.

Tell the truth loudly. Speak to what must change and use your own story—your light— to do so. Darkness won't stand a chance.

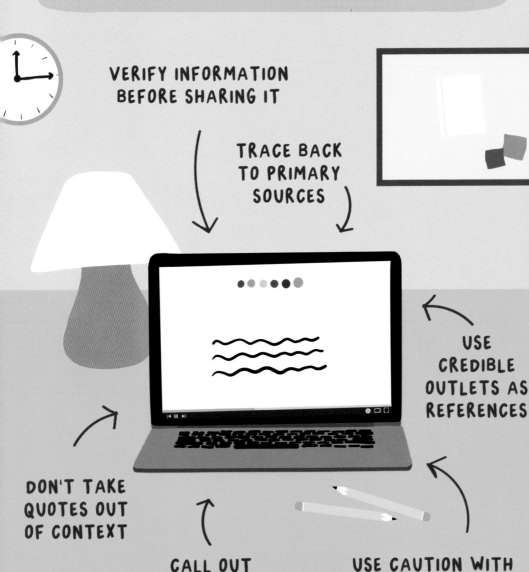

On Truth-Telling

One of our biggest battles in the fight for justice is the battle against misinformation. From fake headlines to exaggerated social media posts, it's easier than ever to be swayed by content purely designed to fan the flames of division. The role of the truth-teller is vital to the preservation of facts and the future of progress.

Truth-tellers are dedicated to verification. They conduct their own research after seeing a trending headline and follow trails to primary sources that are credible and vetted. Before pressing "Share" or "Repost," they do their due diligence because they care about their communities, value being accurate, and want to avoid being conduits of misinformation.

Truth-tellers aren't afraid to call out what's false. They know that their voice has power, and by standing up against lies, they create space for truth to be revealed. Whether it's in online spaces or around the dinner table, they don't let false information go unchallenged, and they are intentional with holding others accountable.

Truth-tellers believe in context. A flashy quote may sound good on its own, but the full scope of the author's words and intent matter more to them than going viral. They know that thoughts and ideas are often accompanied by cultural implications, and that words alone are only part of the full story. They recognize that while some conversations are for everyone, others are intracommunal and are best left to the members of that specific community to engage in.

When gone unchecked, misinformation can cause chaos, diluting—or even derailing—valuable and crucial conversations. Truth-tellers protect facts, history, and stories because they know that the answers to our most pressing questions can be found within them.

NAVIGATING THE TRUTH OF HISTORY

HOW TO LEARN FROM WHAT OUR ANCESTORS LEFT BEHIND

RETRACE THEIR STEPS TO LEARN ABOUT THEIR CHOSEN PATH AND WHY THEY WENT IN THAT DIRECTION

PINPOINT THE PLACES WHERE KEY EVENTS OCCURED TO HAVE CONTEXT ABOUT THE CULTURE OF THE REGION AND THE BELIEFS HELD AT THAT TIME

FIND THEIR NORTH STAR BY DISCOVERING THEIR MOTIVATIONS AND TRUE INTENTIONS

ANALYZE THE BLUEPRINTS OF THEIR DECISIONS AND POLICIES TO UNPACK THE INTRICACIES OF THEIR PLANS

TAKE NOTE OF THE BROADER IMPACTS OF HISTORICAL EVENTS FOR A GREATER SENSE OF THEIR SIGNIFICANCE

The Atlas of the Past

The reluctance to remember our history is rooted in discomfort. There's no pleasure to be found in revisiting our worst moments and camping out in them, excavating truth from the devastation buried deep within. Yet we do it anyway. Like surgery, we cut ourselves open and bleed—not for the fun of it, but to identify what's broken and do the necessary work of repair.

Remembrance aids our understanding of where we are now. Our past contains blueprints, maps, and compasses—tools that explain how we got here and why things unfolded as they did. Dusting off the atlas of the past reveals the mysteries held inside.

One reason to look to history is to gain data that can inform our future decisions. We have years and years of information on what worked and what didn't, and within those experiences we discover what can—and should—be changed.

History also explains how we got here. When examining present-day institutions of injustice, we can follow the trail of history to find out how these systems and structures were handcrafted with intention. When we connect the dots between then and now, our marching orders become much clearer, and we know what must be dismantled.

While the past reminds us of all that went wrong, it also encourages us with the stories of those who worked to get it right. Practicing remembrance is also an act of preservation—aiming to honor those who came before us by telling their stories and refusing to let their legacies be erased.

Failing to bring the truth of history to the light allows hatred and harm to perpetuate in the dark. To ignore the past is to overlook the lessons left in its wake—lessons that mold and shape us into better versions of ourselves and alert us of the long-lasting consequences that still must be dealt with today, on both micro and macro levels. Stewarding our history well is both an honor and a duty.

HEALTHY ACCOUNTABILITY

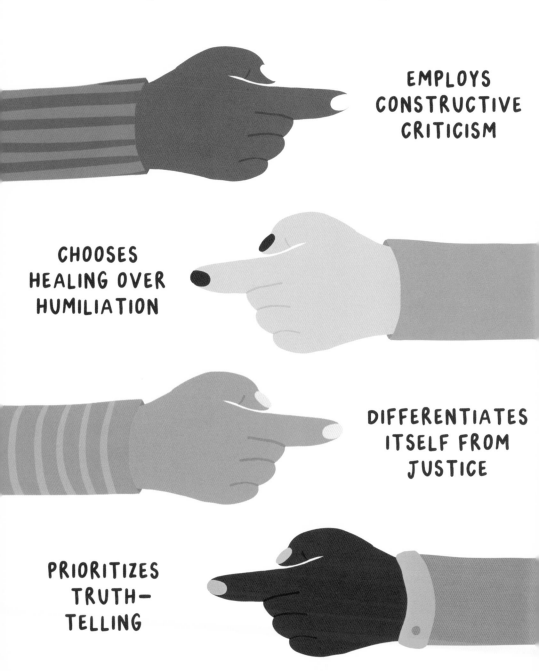

EMPLOYS CONSTRUCTIVE CRITICISM

CHOOSES HEALING OVER HUMILIATION

DIFFERENTIATES ITSELF FROM JUSTICE

PRIORITIZES TRUTH-TELLING

Healthy Accountability

Each of us are responsible for the life we lead. Our decisions leave trails behind us, remnants of the good or evil we choose to pursue. Whether we've asked for it or not, each of us are bound to the concept of accountability: being held responsible for the things we say and do.

While accountability is a positive practice that helps to maintain a standard of morality and justice in our society, it can easily be warped, used as a cloak to disguise poor intentions. As changemakers and doers of good work, it's our job to practice a healthy sense of accountability—one that prioritizes the wholeness and dignity of each person.

Accountability employs constructive criticism. This kind of criticism isn't aimless, solely wielded for the sake of destruction. It has a goal: the improvement of society and justice for all people. In our own lives, we use constructive criticism to build each other up and bring out the best in each other.

Accountability chooses healing over humiliation. Dr. King rejected humiliation in his principles of nonviolence, yet today's accountability culture can sometimes teeter on the edge of nonviolence and violence, seeking to publicly eliminate instead of restore and rehabilitate. Healthy accountability aims for transformation.

Accountability differentiates itself from justice. When an officer is charged with the wrongful killing of an unarmed Black man, that is accountability. When structures are transformed to where Black men aren't at risk of being wrongfully murdered by police, that is justice.

Healthy accountability prioritizes truth-telling and keeps us all committed to the cause of justice. It is our duty to wield it well.

TOUGH PILLS TO SWALLOW

THE TRUTH ABOUT HONESTY

SOMETIMES
IT'S GOOD TO
STIR THE POT

YOU CAN'T
CONTROL HOW
OTHERS REACT

IT CAN BE
UNCOMFORTABLE
BUT NECESSARY

HONESTY
CAN LEAD TO
MUCH-NEEDED
GROWTH FOR YOU
AND OTHERS

AVOIDING THE
TRUTH CAN
PREVENT
PROGRESS

Truth Hurts

There is no way to guarantee that truth-telling lands softly. Like medicine, honest feedback can feel unpleasant on the way down—no matter how many spoonfuls of sugar you send along with it.

While it's most likely never your attention to trigger hurt and pain in someone else, the truth has a way of accomplishing that on its own. Whether you're gearing up for a tough conversation or you're writhing in the guilt of the aftermath, here are a few things to remember about saying hard things with good intentions.

The reactions of others are out of your control.
No matter how hard you try to dress it up or sandwich it between compliments, there's a chance that they'll be offended and react negatively. Rest in the fact that this is a necessary step on the road to change, and although it can be painful, it's worth it.

This is for their good in the end.
Whether the recipient of your truth is a friend, coworker, government official, or social media following, saying hard things with good intentions leads to a higher quality of life for you and others. If you're letting someone know that they've wronged you, they're receiving an opportunity to learn how to love you better. If you're letting them know that they're mistreating themself or others, they're receiving the truth from someone who cares about the ultimate good for them and the people around them.

You are not the problem.
While it may feel like you're the one always pointing things out or stirring the pot, this is how good gets done. Be it for the good of the nation, your circle, or you, speaking up and telling the truth is a necessary step on the path to change.

BE
BOLD
BE
BRAVE

Choosing Boldness

I'm an advocate for choosing a "word of the year." To me, it feels like a low-pressure yet intentional way to look ahead and feel uplifted. When 2019 began, I knew that I wanted to focus on being bold. As someone who sometimes felt overlooked and underestimated, I wanted to encourage myself to tell the truth, choose what was best for me, and pursue my dreams. By the end of that year, I had stood up to a condescending boss, quit my job, let go of a love interest, and started my own business. Safe to say, my boldness paid off.

When you seek to pursue a life of purpose and meaning, boldness will often be required of you. You'll be called on to speak truth to power or say no to opportunities that appear promising but are rooted in toxicity and harm. Courage is not something that must be sought out. It's already within you, lying still like a resting lion. All it takes is the right set of circumstances—a threat to your loved ones, a policy that robs you of your human rights, a dream within reach—to activate that roaring bravery.

Whether a split-second decision or a thoughtfully planned-out strategy, the weight of choosing boldness can feel heavy. Fears will flicker through your mind like a movie, showing you everything that could possibly go wrong. Remember in those moments that you're not living on a whim—you're being guided by an internal compass that consistently points you in the direction that's best for you. When you choose the path of integrity, healing, passion, or another guiding light, you're choosing to be true to who you're made to be. It's this kind of boldness that unlocks the parts of yourself needed to carry out the work you're here to do.

Make those bold choices that your future self will look back on and thank you for.

PEOPLE WHO SPEAK THE TRUTH OUT IN THE OPEN AND DO THE WORK WHEN IT'S TRENDING

PEOPLE WHO DO THE WORK BEHIND CLOSED DOORS AND SPEAK THE TRUTH WHEN IT'S UNPOPULAR

CHANGEMAKERS

When Change Isn't Trending

Much of what we do and discuss each day is dictated by the cycle of a trend. A topic hits the headlines, then we talk about it online and discuss it at dinner. After a few days of watching how it develops and waiting for updates, the topic slowly fades into the background as we move on with life. It's not long before another headline takes its place.

As a changemaker, it's up to you to decide how much of your work will be built on responding to culture versus informing it. There is value to be found in keeping up with what society is discussing, especially when it concerns topics of human rights, policy, and social change. Speaking into the moment with truth will always be needed and valuable. Yet our contribution to culture doesn't end at rebuttals and hot takes.

Changemakers also set the pace. They look at the current conversation and inject truth, but they also find ways to pull out key points and create new topics of discussion. They don't wait for a subject to trend before speaking out on its importance. Informing culture often involves shining a light on what's overlooked and doing the not-so-popular work of planning and organizing for progress.

At the end of the day, much of the change-making work we set out to do is in response to harmful systems already in place. Our collective labor is inherently dictated by what's already happening.

Even so, the work of demolition is rarely limited to the swing of one single wrecking ball in one location. It's the sum of different moments of destroying, dismantling, and removing that occur all throughout the structure, like the several small explosions it takes to bring a building down. We need the people tackling the issues that aren't in the spotlight as much as we need those speaking about what's currently at the center of cultural attention.

The fullness of our work isn't dictated by what's trending but by a lifetime of speaking the truth—even when the masses move on.

DISCOMFORT'S SIGNS

NO MORE HIDING FROM THE TRUTH

CONSIDER NEW PERSPECTIVES

NUANCE ⬇ ONLY

FIND A

NEW WAY ➡

FORWARD

DON'T STOP LEARNING

SLOW DOWN AND SIT WITH THIS

⬅ LOOK ➡

FOR THE LESSON

Getting Uncomfortable

More often than not, embarking on the journey of good work will eventually bring you face-to-face with discomfort. From being asked to interrogate your own biases to being told that you've made a wrong turn, you'll find yourself getting familiar with getting uncomfortable.

At first, these feelings creep in slowly, acting as slow realizations as you process new information. Before long, they sound off in our minds like sirens, setting off triggers of guilt, defeat, or unworthiness. This signals danger for many of us and causes us to halt the process before it truly begins. Perhaps, instead of sending us into shutdown mode or rerouting us altogether, we can train ourselves to have more fruitful reactions to the shock of discomfort.

Instead of signaling danger, think of discomfort as a gentle nudge, notifying you that what you've believed is being challenged and guiding you toward taking the next right step. These nudges move us to ask new questions, like:

"Is this a learning moment for me? What's the lesson here?"
"Do I feel intimidated by this information?"
"Is this dangerous, or just different?"
"Is this person attacking me, or are they holding me accountable?"

Instead of slowing down our journey, discomfort can have us slow down our thought process and sit with new information. Instead of stopping us completely, discomfort can be a reminder to never stop learning. Instead of being a signal to exit the conversation, discomfort can encourage us to change our perspectives and embrace nuance. Instead of making us believe that we're going the wrong way, discomfort can point us in the direction of a new, better way.

Instead of treating discomfort as the end of the road, view it as a pit stop—a pause to reassess and refuel before you journey on.

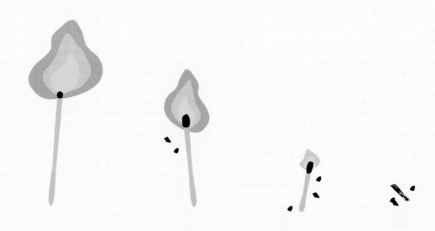

PERFORMATIVE ACTION FIZZLES OUT

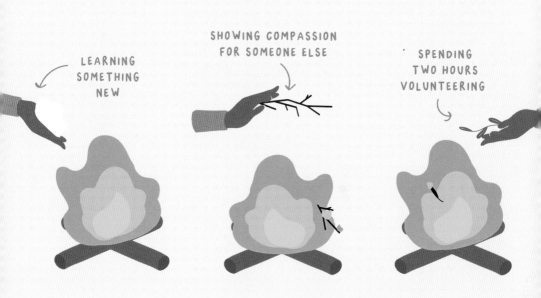

LEARNING SOMETHING NEW

SHOWING COMPASSION FOR SOMEONE ELSE

SPENDING TWO HOURS VOLUNTEERING

A LIFE OF GOOD WORK TENDS THE FLAME

The Allure of Performative Activism

As we trod down the path of progress, there's an alluring side street that calls out for our attention. Lined with bright lights, large billboards, and busy walkways, this street dazzles with spectacle and fanfare. Yet when you wander over to one of these flashy buildings and open the door, you discover that the inside is barren. No people, excitement, or action. It seems that all this street had to offer was the appearance of adventure—with nothing really taking place inside.

Performative activism puts on a show. It dazzles and impresses with its appearance, but beneath the surface, it doesn't have much to offer. We've seen this with thousands of people flocking to follow activists online but soon unfollowing after the excitement died down, or with brands making shiny statements online about change and diversity while their data and C-suites say otherwise.

Staying faithful to the path of progress requires resisting the allure of performative action. Much of the real work that moves things forward happens behind the scenes and in the trenches, not onstage for millions to see. The deciding factor as to whether or not something is performative is not necessarily the action itself but the intent behind it. We assess our own intent by asking, "Am I doing this to be seen, or to actively support the community I'm standing with?"

Performative action fizzles out. While often approached with good intentions, it's also sometimes spurred on by pressure to gain attention or avoid being "canceled." It appears powerful but lacks the planning, investment, and tenacity to see it through past a short period of time. Good work acknowledges that while it may not always be glamorous or captivating, it's most certainly the main attraction and worthy of sustained effort.

Being Honest with Yourself

How are you doing? Honestly?

Take inventory of life for a moment. What kind of difficulties are you currently facing? From short-term challenges like overwhelming deadlines to long-term challenges like grief, we're consistently trying to stay afloat as we battle life's winds and waves. The good work we aim to do in the world is highly affected by the challenges we face in our personal lives, and our own well-being depends on us dealing with that reality.

Living a life of meaningful impact requires being honest with ourselves. Personal honesty prevents us from overwhelming ourselves with doing too much too soon. Two aspects of life that are helpful to be consistently aware of are the season you find yourself in and the extent of your knowledge.

Someone once told me that they wish they could do "more" good work in the world around them, but their time was currently dedicated to taking care of their mother who was battling a terminal illness. If you're in the middle of dealing with devastating loss, struggling mental health, or any other situation that weighs heavily on you, then it's completely permissible—and honestly, critical—to dedicate your time to your own well-being. *You* are as good a cause to invest in as anything else, and your capacity to do good in the world around you heavily depends on your ability to live well.

Another part of personal honesty involves analyzing the extent of your knowledge. It's common to be tempted to dive headfirst into "taking action" without honestly assessing what you know and what's needed from you. Resist the temptation to appoint yourself as the resident expert in an area that may already have qualified leaders taking charge. Instead, see how you can join in or learn from those who have been actively engaged and present.

Being honest with yourself ensures that you're doing the best you can with what you have. Whatever that may be in this season, that's more than enough.

REDEM

PTION

TODAY IS A <u>GOOD DAY</u> TO BEGIN AGAIN, TO KEEP MOVING FORWARD, AND TO CELEBRATE HOW FAR YOU'VE COME

Begin Again

You are allowed to begin again. The journey of good work has no apex; there is no pinnacle or highest point. There are only hills and valleys—moments of great joy as we progress and moments of deep sorrow when we fail. Imperfection is inevitable, but you can always begin again.

You are a product of your environment. The worldview you hold today is a reflection of your upbringing, experiences, and surroundings. The gift that growth brings is the ability to tear away the harmful ideologies or practices that you may find yourself wrapped up in, opening yourself up to the beauty of new beginnings.

There is no condemnation for you here. What good comes of wallowing in the shame of a past that cannot be changed? Shed your old perspectives like a tree sheds its leaves in the fall, knowing that after a season, new ones will sprout to replace them. Tend to your soil. Weed out all that is not welcome.

To be redeemed is to be freed from the things that cause harm or distress. It's a process of restoration, exchanging old for new. Surely, the evils of racism, hate, and apathy are weeds that need to be uprooted—they take hold in the soil of our hearts and choke out the good in us. They rob us of the gift of growth by blocking the light of truth.

Pruning can often feel like destroying. Cutting away the parts of us that inhibit our collective healing is a process of dying to self. Yet we have an opportunity to replace what we've lost with newness and beauty by cultivating the good within us. Choose love, empathy, curiosity, and consistency. Allow yourself to be challenged in conversation, awakened through literature, and sharpened in community. In time, you'll bear new fruit.

TRUE REDEMPTION	FALSE REDEMPTION
seeks to restore wholeness	seeks to return to dysfunction
moves toward progress	maintains the status quo
acknowledges history	repeats history
atones for mistakes	evades accountability
reforms harmful systems	revives harmful systems

A Twisted Redemption

If there's one thing that history teaches us, it's that progress ebbs and flows. With any meaningful lunge toward positive change, an inevitable backlash takes place, seeking to thwart our best efforts and push us backward.

The pages of history books tell this story. We're told of a time called Reconstruction, a period after the Civil War when newly freed Black Americans started taking steps toward equal standing in society through citizenship and political participation. What followed, however, was a calculated and widespread attack on these efforts known as the "Redemption." Those who opposed Black progress engaged in white supremacist domestic terrorism throughout the South, eventually halting hopes for free and equitable coexistence. Eventually, Jim Crow segregation would take its place, ushering in a new—yet familiar—wave of injustice.

This, of course, is not the kind of redemption we seek to practice as doers of good work. This twisted redemption does not seek reform or positive change, but rather a return to the harmful oppressive systems that make opponents of progress most comfortable. Instead of hopeful restoration and renewed hearts, it fights the work of improving society by maintaining the status quo. This "redemption" will not free us.

History has a way of repeating itself. Today, we see false redemption try to weasel its way into political offices, school board meetings, and holiday dinner tables. Those who've opposed the progress of racial justice seek to combat it by banning novels and rewriting history books. Elected officials fan the flames of hate with violent rhetoric. Still, history also shows us that we are not without hope.

Change is possible when we decide that moving forward toward human flourishing and true redemption is a worthy pursuit.

FOR-
GIVE
FOR
YOU

Forgive for You

I'm sorry for what happened to you.

That hurtful remark or traumatic incident swooped in and sought to muffle your voice and smother your light. It knocked the wind out of you, piercing your heart and causing you great pain.

Unforgiveness is a prison of your own design. Every passing moment soaked in bitterness and resentment becomes a link on the chain binding you to this part of your story. The episode plays again and again in your mind, trapping you in a loop of devastation and despair. Yet even here, freedom is waiting.

Forgiveness is not for them. It's for you.

The people who hurt you do not have to live with the replay of what happened in the way that you do. You are worthy of the peace that comes with release. Even if you do not forget, you can let go and begin the journey of healing. This bondage is holding you back from experiencing life in its fullness, and you are worthy of fully feeling the joy and beauty of every good thing meant for you. It is not too late to redeem and reclaim your time.

Good exists on the other side of this. It may look like fully healing from the experience and walking in liberty. It could also involve using your story of how you overcame as comfort and inspiration for someone else who may now be walking in the shoes you once wore. Either way, exchanging the chains of resentment for the freedom of forgiveness will release you into a future full of hope and possibility.

CLARITY LAYS ALL THE
CARDS ON THE TABLE

AMBIGUITY HIDES ITS HAND

Clarity and Restoration

Clarity isn't often explicitly viewed as restorative. We know it to be helpful when it sheds light on issues we face, or a time-saver when it gives more context for projects. However, we are more familiar with the feeling of frustration that accompanies a lack of clarity in relationships, jobs, or the pursuit of change. Yet when we choose the bravery of tough, clear conversations over avoidance or ambiguity, we set the stage for real transformation to take place.

To begin with, clarity provides an honest assessment of a situation that lights the path of problem-solving. In moments where two parties seek restoration, clarity puts all the cards on the table and shows all hands. It illuminates every crack and crevice, leaving nothing open to interpretation and honestly demonstrating what we're working with. This type of honesty allows everyone to have the same starting point, making it easier to move toward solutions.

Clarity also enables truth-telling that clears the way. When embarking on the path toward healing and restoration, truth-telling points out bumps in the road and potential hazards. With a clear perspective on what's causing harm, we can more accurately attack issues head-on and remove roadblocks to progress.

A third gift that clarity gives us is the vulnerability that enables us to move forward in wholeness and truth. When we honestly assess a situation and tell the truth about what hinders progress, we're opening ourselves up by sharing our own hopes, needs, and desires. The bravery of vulnerability lies in the way we put ourselves out there and our willingness to be honest about the effects of the ways we've been hurt or the ways we've hurt others.

Clarity does not come without risks, but it is accompanied by the reward of transparent relationships, clearer next steps, and the courage to be open enough to let light in.

DO JUSTICE

LOVE MERCY

WALK HUMBLY

MICAH 6:8

Upward, Inward, Outward

As someone with a happy and hopeful artistic voice who tackles hard and heavy topics, I'm often asked for the method behind the work I do. There are those who wonder what keeps me dedicated to these topics and how I maintain a hopeful disposition when working for change often leaves us exhausted and disappointed, so I thought I'd share what keeps me centered and whole in this difficult work.

As a person of faith, I adopted my framework for good work from biblical principles, but these ideals can be widely applied to everyone. It involves three concepts: justice, mercy, and humility. Humility is largely tied to my faith system and view of God. I maintain that I am a recipient of redemption, and this upward focus drives me to love my neighbor as I, myself, am loved. Each of us has worth and dignity, and loving each other well is not optional.

The other two concepts, justice and mercy, are often seen as opposites. Yet it's the balance of the two that causes me to pursue justice while focusing on restoration and to prioritize mercy while valuing accountability.

Mercy is an inward focus. It involves consistently fighting against bitterness, choosing forgiveness, and showing compassion to others. A dedication to mercy keeps me soft, reminding me that all of us are flawed and are often in need of mercy ourselves.

Justice is the outward focus, the concept that often gets the most attention in this work—and rightly so. I acknowledge that justice is a continuum of all that is fair and right, and it's my duty to ensure that my neighbor's access to it is not cut off. Doing justice involves repairing harm, advocating for equity, and ensuring that people are treated fairly.

When combined, the pursuits of justice, mercy, and humility exist in a delicate balance that keeps me grounded, dedicated, and focused on what matters most.

THE GOALS OF REPARATIONS

BASED ON RECOMMENDATIONS BY THE UNITED NATIONS

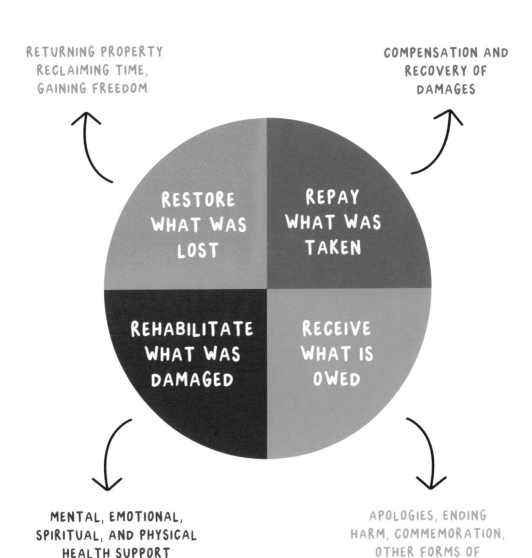

RETURNING PROPERTY
RECLAIMING TIME,
GAINING FREEDOM

COMPENSATION AND
RECOVERY OF
DAMAGES

RESTORE WHAT WAS LOST

REPAY WHAT WAS TAKEN

REHABILITATE WHAT WAS DAMAGED

RECEIVE WHAT IS OWED

MENTAL, EMOTIONAL,
SPIRITUAL, AND PHYSICAL
HEALTH SUPPORT

APOLOGIES, ENDING
HARM, COMMEMORATION,
OTHER FORMS OF
ACKNOWLEDGMENT

On Reparations

When we mess up, it's in our nature to attempt to make amends. We pay the cost of repair for a broken item, send a bouquet of flowers to express heartfelt apologies, or make space to have serious conversations and get to the root of why the harm occurred in the first place. As a country, America is no stranger to messing up. From forced displacement and colonialism to slavery and internment, there is much in our history that requires the attempt to make amends in some way, even though the deep-seated trauma caused by these events and others cannot be reversed or fully healed.

This idea is tied to the concept of reparations, defined by the United Nations as "measures to redress violations of human rights by providing a range of material and symbolic benefits to victims or their families as well as affected communities." We've heard this term used widely in reference to monetary compensation, like when Japanese American survivors of internment received $20,000 each, but this concept is far much more than that.

As a whole, reparations acknowledge the fact that there are widespread, complex, and deeply ingrained consequences for our actions. When you trace the roots of modern-day issues affecting historically oppressed communities back through time, you see that many systemic injustices are directly related to racism, colonialism, and white supremacy. The economic, relational, mental, and educational costs of this are high. The concept of reparations acknowledges that there is much work to be done to help restore lives, rehabilitate minds, and end ongoing systems that perpetuate these injustices.

Acknowledging the magnitude of our wrongs illuminates all we must do to make things right. While we, as individuals, may not be the direct cause of present-day oppression, we have a beautiful opportunity to take steps to alleviate the suffering of those around us by doing what we can to make amends—systemically and individually. This is the cost of redemptive, restorative love.

When Justice Restores

There is a light within each of us. We begin life with wide, open eyes, taking in all that we see and stumbling forward into the unknown. Before long, we're met with life's difficulties. We become formed and shaped by what happens to us, and that formation affects how we treat others. It can seem like life does all it can to blow out that light within us.

Restorative justice takes this light into account when seeking to repair harm. It opens a space of healing for the person who was harmed, while also remembering the dignity of the person who caused it. It creates room for voices to be heard, impact to be acknowledged, and change to take place.

This differs from systems of administering justice that focus solely on punishment, often called retributive justice. We are more than the sum of our worst mistakes, and many could benefit from being given the opportunity to address underlying issues that may have led to those things. This doesn't mean that people aren't held accountable for the harm they have caused and the consequences of those decisions. Alternatively, the restorative approach recognizes that some people are less likely to continue perpetuating cycles of harm when they're treated for the root cause of it.

There are many reasons why the light within someone may flicker or grow dim. Choosing the path of restoration recognizes the dignity of a person, the importance of community, and the value of focusing on ending overall cycles of harm.

CALLING OUT OR CALLING IN?

A GUIDE TO NAVIGATING EACH APPROACH

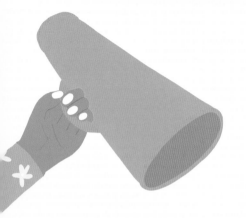

CALLING OUT

ACTIVE HARM IS TAKING PLACE AND NEEDS TO BE INTERRUPTED

ATTEMPTS TO CALL THEM IN HAVE BEEN INEFFECTIVE

CALLING IN COULD POTENTIALLY BE UNSAFE

THE PERSON OR GROUP IS EXHIBITING A HARMFUL PATTERN UNAPOLOGETICALLY

CALLING IN

THERE'S A DESIRE TO CREATE A SMALLER OR MORE PRIVATE ENVIRONMENT

A PERSONAL RELATIONSHIP OR ESTABLISHED CONNECTION EXISTS

PRIORITIZES AN OPPORTUNITY FOR LEARNING AND GROWTH

THE SITUATION ISN'T AS URGENT OR UNSAFE

Calling In, Calling Out

We are all human, prone to cause harm in one way or another. When you bring a group of imperfect people together, no matter the intention, hurt is sure to follow. The ideas of "calling in" and "calling out" are two different plans of action for identifying individuals or groups causing harm and bringing their behavior to their attention.

Contrary to popular belief, "calling out" isn't the evil twin sister of "calling in." Both processes are necessary, and both serve their purpose in different ways. When harm is actively taking place and a person or group needs to immediately put an end to their behavior, a call-out involves naming the harm, defending the recipient of it, and calling for an end to it. Call-outs can happen anywhere, from a town hall meeting to a conversation at home. Regardless of where it takes place and who is at fault, the aim isn't humiliation but urgent accountability that prevents continued harm.

Call-ins are normally more private and personal in nature. It focuses on connection, relationships, and creating a safe space for dialogue. Its conversational nature is the perfect fit for discussions that aren't as urgent or public-facing, but still need to be addressed.

Regardless of the approach, the end goal is reconciliation. Progress is a communal cause, and we hinder our own efforts when we choose to shame or embarrass those who are on this journey with us. Even if the wrongdoer intended to harm us, we do not win when we mirror the harmful behaviors of those who perpetuate unjust systems.

When your next opportunity to speak out against harm presents itself, remember the humanity in each of us and let your response reflect the good you wish to see.

The Olive Branch

I've spent the majority of my life being conflict averse. I value easy, peaceful friendships, and in past instances where a friendship started to fizzle out, I was more likely to count my losses than rekindle the flame. I'm a work in progress, but to this day, my significant other is much more likely to be the first to apologize than I am. I've often found myself more willing to exist in inner turmoil than to extend an olive branch.

Extending an olive branch is initiating a process of peace, goodwill, and reconciliation. If you're anything like me, this isn't the easiest process to start. In instances of disagreement or healthy conflict, being willing to bury the hatchet and make amends is a sign of humility.

When mustering up the strength to take that first step, remember the love you share with the other person or group of people. That love involves wishing and working for their well-being, and that may sometimes look like being the first to apologize. It may also be helpful to ponder on the value of the relationship(s) and how much they mean to you. Ask yourself:

"Do they have my best interest at heart?"
"Are we still on the same page in terms of intent, values, and how we view this relationship?"
"Are each of us committed to growth and progress?"
"Is there mutual respect?"

Relationships are the most valuable parts of our lives. We build each other up, offer mutual support, and change the world together. When a relationship is safe, life-giving, and fruitful, it may be worth the work it takes to protect it.

OUTER WORK
IS MOMENTARY,
MORE DIFFICULT,
AND LESS
IMPACTFUL

OUTER WORK
IS A NATURAL
OUTFLOW WITH
LONGEVITY AND
DEEPER MEANING

INNER WORK
LEFT UNDONE

INNER WORK
IN PROGRESS

BEHAVIOR
MODIFICATION
FOCUSES ON
EXTERNAL ACTION

REDEMPTIVE
TRANSFORMATION
FOCUSES ON INTERNAL
CHANGE

The Fruit of Redemption

What is the proof of a life transformed? It cannot be found in spoken words, however lovely or truthful they may appear, for it is far too easy to be deceived by them. It cannot be measured by a few good deeds, however well-meaning, for there is no guarantee that they'll continue beyond a moment. True transformation begins with a changed heart.

A changed heart doesn't occur of our own free will. It wasn't until the Grinch witnessed the tenacious goodwill of the citizens of Whoville that his heart grew three sizes, causing him to leave behind his past of evil deeds and walk in redemption. This kind of inner renewal only takes place after a heart encounters the power of all that is good, right, and true, giving in to its beckoning and opening up the door.

What comes next is a changed mind. Once exposed to the light of truth and the power of a new heart, the transformed person adopts a new perspective. Harmful beliefs are released, freeing up space in the mind for updated information. No longer trapped in their old thought patterns, the renewed mind flourishes as it gains new knowledge.

A new heart and new mind combine to produce changed behavior. This differs from temporary behavior modification because it is not limited to momentary bursts of will. Unlike performative good deeds that eventually wither and fade because they have no roots, the transformed person's behavior is sustained by its connection to the sources of a renewed mind and heart.

What is the proof of a life transformed? Only time will tell. But, if tended to and cultivated, redemption bears the fruit of changed minds, hearts, and deeds.

About the Author

Danielle Coke Balfour is a designer turned illustrator, advocate, speaker, and entrepreneur. She's the founder of Oh Happy Dani, a lifestyle brand and educational platform that uses artwork and resources to encourage empathy, inspire justice, and make complex ideas more accessible. She's driven by her desire to help everyday advocates do good daily in their spheres of influence using their passions and skills, and she's fostered a community of over half a million people across social media. With a joy that flows from her desire to love her neighbor as herself, Danielle hopes to spark action in pursuit of the ultimate good as you hold her art in your home and carry it in your heart.

Acknowledgments

To my agent, Annette Bourland, and the team at Andrews McMeel, thank you for fighting for my work, amplifying my voice, and letting me pour my heart onto these pages.

Andrews McMeel Publishing
a division of Andrews McMeel Universal
1130 Walnut Street, Kansas City, Missouri 64106

www.andrewsmcmeel.com

23 24 25 26 27 SDB 10 9 8 7 6 5 4 3 2 1

ISBN: 978-1-5248-8122-1

Library of Congress Control Number: 2023934775

Editor: Patty Rice
Art Director: Julie Barnes
Designer: Tiffany Meairs
Production Editor: David Shaw
Production Manager: Tamara Haus

ATTENTION: SCHOOLS AND BUSINESSES

Andrews McMeel books are available at quantity discounts with bulk purchase for educational, business, or sales promotional use. For information, please e-mail the Andrews McMeel Publishing Special Sales Department: sales@amuniversal.com.